A Precept Bible Study for Home Groups

Philippians:
Rejoice in the Lord

A Verse-by-Verse Journey through Philippians

Ralph Robert Gomez

WESTBOW
PRESS®
A DIVISION OF THOMAS NELSON
& ZONDERVAN

ISBN: 979-8-3850-0688-5 (sc)
ISBN: 979-8-3850-0689-2 (e)

Library of Congress Control Number: 2023917118

Scripture quotations taken from the (NASB®)
New American Standard Bible®, Copyright © 1960, 1971, 1977,
1995, 2020 by The Lockman Foundation.
Used by permission.
All rights reserved. www.lockman.org.

Scripture quotations marked NLT are taken from the Holy Bible, New
Living Translation, copyright © 1996, 2004, 2007.

Scripture quotations taken from the NIV®
(New International Version®), Copyright ©1973, 1978, 1984, 2011 by Biblica, Inc.™
Used by permission of Zondervan.
All rights reserved worldwide. www.zondervan.com.
The "NIV" and "New International Version" are trademarks registered
in the United States Patent and Trademark Office by Biblica, Inc.™

Scripture quotations marked MSG are taken from THE MESSAGE,
copyright © 1993, 2002, 2018 by Eugene H. Peterson.
Used by permission of NavPress,
represented by Tyndale House Publishers. All rights reserved.

A special thank you to GotQuestions.org for the content,
as it was of great benefit to me in writing this book.

Disclaimer

The views and conclusions of this study guide are based on the author's in-depth study of Philippians.
The author understands that others may come to different conclusions based on their own study.

All scripture quotations are taken from the NASB® unless otherwise marked.
Emphasis has been added throughout the book.

WestBow Press
1663 Liberty Drive
Bloomington, IN 47403
www.westbowpress.com
844-714-3454
A Division of Thomas Nelson & Zondervan

Print information available on the last page.

WestBow Press rev. date: 09/18/2023

PRAISE FOR
PHILIPPIANS: REJOICE IN THE LORD

I recently finished the precept Bible study on Philippians written by Ralph Gomez and would highly recommend it to anyone that wants to start a small group Bible study. It is simple to understand and the "reflective questions" invoke group interaction that keeps everyone engaged in fruitful conversation. I have taught many Bible studies and this is by far one of the best formats that I have seen and used. Ralph methodically breaks down each verse and highlights the most important aspects of the text. Each section is divided into "bite size pieces" so as not to overwhelm the reader. He brings the reader full circle at the end of each study with the re-read section which I really like. You can't miss what God has to say...it is laid out so succinctly and comprehensively. Read it, enjoy it and do it! Your life will be blessed and your small group will flourish! I will be looking forward to seeing what Ralph has in-store for us next!

STEVE MORAN
Associate Pastor
Word Alive Church
Thornton, CO

CONTENTS

ACKNOWLEDGMENTS

I want to thank the members of the *James Gang Home Group* and the *Band of Brothers Men's Group* for all their love and support. I especially want to thank my wife, Marlene, who encouraged me to follow my passion, as well as the many pastors and spiritual teachers who have mentored me over the years.

I want to thank my Lord and Savior for His grace and mercy. I was thirty-nine years old when He lifted the scales from my eyes, allowing me to see the truth. It just goes to show that no matter how young or old you are, God will never give up on you. I am living proof that God will leave the ninety-nine sheep and pursue the one lost sheep. *Thank you, Jesus!*

I do not consider myself a biblical scholar. However, I have tried to capture the insight and wisdom from the many friends and family who have participated in our home groups over the years. Their contribution has been invaluable in putting this study together. My hope is if you are a Christian, this Bible study will reignite your passion for God's Word; and if you are a seeker, my hope and prayer is that God will use this study to woo you into His family. It does not matter how far away you have drifted or what you have done; God loves you and is waiting for you to make a move.

If you are ready to repent and give your life to Jesus, I encourage you to do it now. As the Apostle Paul said to the Corinthians, "*TODAY is the day of salvation.*" If you are ready to take this step, may I suggest a simple prayer from the Reverend Billy Graham?

> "*Dear Lord Jesus, I know that I am a sinner, and I ask for Your forgiveness. I believe You died for my sins and rose from the dead. I turn from my sins and invite You to come into my heart and life. I want to trust and follow You as my Lord and Savior. In Your name, amen.*"

If you have said this prayer and believe it in your heart, may I be the first to welcome you into the family of God. Find yourself a Bible-teaching church and plug in. In time, I hope you'll come to love your new church family as much as I do mine.

INTRODUCTION

This is an **eight-week study** on the Apostle Paul's letter to the believers in Philippi. The Philippian church was started during Paul's second missionary journey when he led a women named Lydia and a Philippian jailer to the Lord. Fast forward ten years and we find Paul on house arrest in Rome for a crime he did not commit. Paul wrote Philippians to thank them for their financial support and encouragement. He also used this letter to address an issue that was threatening to divide the church.

Philippians has been described as Paul's joy letter because it emphasizes the joy of living the Christian life. What makes this letter so remarkable is that Paul was joyful and found contentment while wrongfully imprisoned in Rome. How is this possible? Listen to Paul's answer: "*I have learned to be content in whatever circumstances I am. I know how to get along with little, and I also know how to live in prosperity; in any and every circumstance I have learned the secret of being filled and going hungry, both of having abundance and suffering need*" (Philippians 4:11-12).

What was Paul's secret for being content and living a joyful life no matter his circumstances? His secret was simple, it was grounded in his faith in Jesus. That's what this study is about. Join me as we follow Paul and experience the special relationship he had with the Philippians and his deep desire to know Christ above all else.

How to Use This Study

This study guide is designed for 8-12 people, and each weekly study should take approximately 60-70 minutes to complete. There are two sections in the study. The odd-numbered pages are the study guides, and the even-numbered pages contain the answers to the study guide questions. Therefore, you don't need to be an expert on the Bible to facilitate a group; you just need to have a desire and a willingness to draw closer to God and to other believers. Keep in mind, as the facilitator, your main responsibility is to start and stop the group on time, and to keep the discussion on track as well as to encourage everyone to participate.

The study is arranged so that everyone has the opportunity to participate by reading a section and then answering the questions from that section. The end of each section is marked by a solid black line that says

`Stop and discuss the above`

At this point, the reader can choose to answer the questions or pass. After the reader has answered the questions or passed, the discussion is then opened up to the group. Once the group discussion for that section has completed, the facilitator or reader should read the answers on the back of the next page.

Then the next person reads the ensuing section. This continues in round-robin style until the entire study has been read. The end of the study is designated with "**Let's RE-Read Tonight's Verses.**"

In this section, each person reads to the ~~~~~ separator and then rotates readers until the entire chapter has been read. This is a very important step and should not be skipped. It is amazing how the Holy Spirit will bring a new level of understanding after the entire chapter has been studied verse by verse and then re-read in its entirety.

Group Guidelines

1. Silence all cell phones.

2. Stay focused and set aside outside factors.

3. Give the group your full attention.

4. Encourage everyone to participate and to ask questions.

5. No one person should dominate the discussion; everyone's input matters.

6. What is said in the group, stays in the group. Confidentiality is a must.

7. Each group should start and end with prayer.

8. Have fun!

Philippians:
Rejoice in the Lord

WEEK 1 - PHILIPPIANS 1:1-11

Notes

Let's Review Tonight's Study

Philippians was co-written by the Apostle Paul and Timothy to the churches in Philippi about ten years after Paul's second missionary journey. Paul went to Philippi after receiving a vision in Troas to come to Macedonia. When he got to Philippi he led a jailer and a woman named Lydia to Christ. After Paul left, Lydia opened her house up for believers to meet and this eventually became the first church in Philippi (Acts 16:11-35).

Paul wrote this letter to thank the Philippians for their financial support and encouragement. He also used this letter to address an issue between two women that was threatening to divide the church. The theme of this letter is joy, and it expresses Paul's deep love and friendship for the Philippians. What makes this letter so remarkable is that despite his wrongful imprisonment, he was full of joy. Philippians is one of the four letters commonly referred to as the Prison Epistles. The other three Prison Epistles are: Ephesians, Colossians, and Philemon.

The chart below shows a timeline of all of Paul's letters, and where he was when he wrote them. Paul wrote thirteen letters in the New Testament.

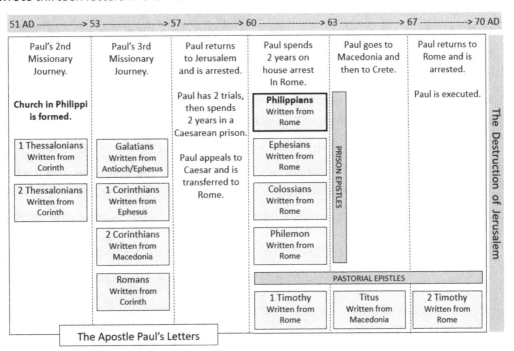

As you read this letter, you'll see that Paul had a special friendship with the Philippians that went far beyond the typical pastor relationship. We also know from our study on the book of Acts that Paul and Timothy had a special friendship as well.

Reflective Question: *Am I a friend that is reliable and can be trusted? Do I keep my promises?*

(Q) WHAT IS THE DIFFERENCE BETWEEN HAVING A *"FRIENDSHIP"* AND BEING AN *"ACQUAINTANCE"*?
_____

(Q) ANY MORE COMMENTS? _____

Stop and discuss the above comments and questions — Answer to questions are on the next page.

Answers to Questions from the Previous Page

(Q) WHAT IS THE DIFFERENCE BETWEEN HAVING A *"FRIENDSHIP"* AND BEING AN *"ACQUAINTANCE"*?

FRIENDSHIP

- The dictionary defines friendship as a close relationship between two people sharing common interest, morals, values, and is based on trust and loyalty.

- Friends can be care-free around each other and will confide with one another with complete trust.

- Friends contribute to the emotional well-being of each other.

- Friends respect and encourage one another.

- Friends make time to see each other and can be counted on in good times and in bad times.

- The ultimate friendship is found in the Gospel of John when Jesus said, *"Greater love has no one than this, that a person will lay down his life for his friends"* (John 15:13).

ACQUAINTANCE

- The dictionary defines an acquaintance as someone you may know but do not have a close friendship with.

- An acquaintance might be someone you see every day but do not share personal details of your life with. Conversations are shallow and superficial.

- An acquaintance might be a co-worker, business associate or a friend of a friend.

- An acquaintance might be someone you are meeting for the first time. You might greet them with "It's nice to make your acquaintance."

- Over time, an acquaintance may turn into a friendship.

Let's Begin Tonight's Study

Philippians 1:1a (NASB). [1] Paul and Timothy, **bondservant**s of Christ Jesus.

Commentary. Paul opened this letter by identifying Timothy and himself as co-authors and *"bondservants of Christ."* The Greek word for bondservant is **Doulos** which means someone who belongs to another and has no rights of their own, or someone who has voluntarily given up their rights to serve their master. By describing themselves as bondservants, Paul and Timothy were saying they have chosen to serve Jesus for the rest of their lives and belong to Him. Jesus said, *"If anyone wants to come after Me, he must deny himself, take up his cross, and follow Me"* (Matthew 16:24). Paul became a Doulos when he walked away from his old life as a Pharisee in the upper ranks of Judaism to follow Jesus. He was beaten numerous times and almost died on several occasions, and yet he persevered and remained faithful to his calling.

Reflective Question: Am I a Doulos? Have I laid down "my rights" so that I can serve God in ALL areas of my life?

What about Timothy? We know that Paul met Timothy as a young boy during his first missionary journey through Galatia. A few years later when Paul came through Lystra during his second missionary journey, Timothy joined Paul, Silas and Luke as they traveled north to Philippi.

(Q) WHAT ELSE DO YOU KNOW ABOUT TIMOTHY? _____

(Q) ANY COMMENTS ON THESES VERSES? _____

Stop and discuss the above comments and questions — Answer to questions are on the next page.

Philippians 1:1b (NASB). To all the **saints** in Christ Jesus who are in Philippi.

Commentary. Paul referred to the believers in Philippi as *"saints."* According to the dictionary, saint means a person of exceptional holiness or goodness. Some people might even say a saint is a perfect person without sin. If you were raised a Catholic, you have been taught that saints are people who have died and been canonized by the Pope. Is this supported by the Bible? Let's take a look.

The Hebrew word for saint is **Hagios** which means to be set apart by God. All Christians have been set apart by God because of the **righteousness** they received when Jesus atoned for their sins on the cross. In other words, the Bible refers to ALL Christians as saints. How is this possible? If saint means a person of exceptional holiness or goodness, how can people born into sin be called saints?

(Q) HOW DOES GOD'S RIGHTEOUSNESS MAKE A BELIEVER A SAINT? _____

(Q) ANY COMMENTS ON THESES VERSES? _____

Stop and discuss the above comments and questions — Answer to questions are on the next page.

Answers to Questions from the Previous Page

(Q) WHAT ELSE DO YOU KNOW ABOUT TIMOTHY?

- His father was Greek and his mother was Jewish (2 Timothy 1:5).

- Since he was a mixed race, Timothy was able to relate to both the Greeks and the Jews when sharing the gospel.

- Paul met Timothy during his first missionary journey through Galatia (Acts 16:1).

- Timothy traveled with Paul on his second missionary journey (Acts chapter 16).

- Paul mentored Timothy and led him to the Lord (2 Timothy 3:10-15).

- Paul loved Timothy like his own son and served as a spiritual father to him (2 Timothy 1:2).

- Timothy had a passion for reaching the lost and even allowed Paul to circumcise him so that he would be more effective when sharing the gospel with Jews (Acts 16:1-3).

- Timothy was timid and struggled with his youthfulness (1 Timothy 4:12).

- Paul wrote two letters to Timothy to encourage him. These letters are called the pastoral epistles.

- Paul sent Timothy to several churches to represent him when he wasn't able to go (1 Corinthians 4:17; Philippians 2:19, 1 Thessalonians 3:2).

- Timothy was the pastor of the church at Ephesus (1 Timothy 1:3).

- Timothy had a chronic illness (1 Timothy 5:23).

- Timothy co-wrote three letters with Paul (Philippians 1:1, 1 Thessalonians 1:1, Philemon 1:1).

(Q) HOW DOES GOD'S RIGHTEOUSNESS MAKE A BELIEVER A SAINT?

- First of all, God is a perfect being without sin.

- Secondly, everyone is born into sin because of the fall of Adam and Eve in the Garden of Eden. Therefore, no one can enter heaven because of their sin and there is nothing anyone can do to earn their way into heaven.

What hope is there for sinners?

- When Jesus went to the cross, He took on the sins of the world and purchased salvation for all who repent and place their faith in Him. As the Bible says, "*He made Him who knew no sin to be sin in our behalf,* ***so that we might become the righteousness of God in Him***" (2 Corinthians 5:21).

- What this means is all believers are positionally righteous even though they still sin because God has credited the righteousness of Jesus Christ to their account. Christians are not righteous in and of their selves; rather, they enjoy Christ's righteousness that was applied to their account.

- Therefore, all Christians are saints in the eyes of God because of the righteousness of Jesus Christ.

> **Philippians 1:1c (NASB).** To all the saints in Christ Jesus who are in Philippi, including the **overseers** and **deacons**.

Commentary. After Paul introduced himself and Timothy, he greeted the believers in Philippi, including the overseers and deacons. Who are the overseers and deacons? These are leadership positions in the church which Paul described in his first letter to Timothy. Here are the **requirements**.

- *"An **overseer**, must be above reproach, the husband of one wife, temperate, self-controlled, respectable, hospitable, skillful in teaching, not overindulging in wine, not a bully, but gentle, not contentious, free from the love of money. He must be one who manages his own household well, keeping his children under control with all dignity (but if a man does not know how to manage his own household, how will he take care of the church of God?) and not a new convert, so that he will not become conceited and fall into condemnation incurred by the devil. And he must have a good reputation with those outside the church, so that he will not fall into disgrace and the snare of the devil"* (1 Timothy 3:2-7).

- *"A **deacon** must be men of dignity, not insincere, not prone to drink much wine, or greedy for money, but holding to the mystery of the faith with a clear conscience. These men must also first be tested; then have them serve as deacons if they are beyond reproach"* (1 Timothy 3:8-10).

If these are the requirements for overseers and deacons, what are their **responsibilities**?

- An **overseer** is a pastor or an elder. In some translations they are called bishops. Overseers serve the church by leading, teaching, praying, counseling, etc. The book of Acts warns overseers to *"be on guard for yourselves and for all the flock, among which the Holy Spirit has made you overseers, to shepherd the church of God"* (Acts 20:28).

- A **deacon** is a worker who serves in the church and may be responsible for things like: managing the sound system, or volunteering in the children's ministry, or serving as a greeter, or cleaning the building, etc. In other words, a deacon is a servant. We find the first deacons in the book of Acts where *"the twelve [apostles] summoned the congregation of the disciples and said, 'It is not desirable for us to neglect the word of God in order to serve tables. Instead, brothers and sisters, select from among you seven men of good reputation, full of the Spirit and of wisdom, whom we may put in charge of this task'"* (Acts 6:2-3).

Overseers, deacons, bishops and servants follow the **Moses Model** for church leadership. The Moses Model was used during the 40 years the Israelites were lost in the desert (Exodus 18).

(Q) WHAT IS THE *"MOSES MODEL"* FOR CHURCH LEADERSHIP? _____

(Q) ANY COMMENTS ON THESES VERSES? _____

Stop and discuss the above comments and questions — Answer to questions are on the next page.

Answers to Questions from the Previous Page

(Q) WHAT IS THE "*MOSES MODEL*" FOR CHURCH LEADERSHIP?

- This management style is based on the leadership structure that Moses implemented in the Old Testament to divide the workload (Exodus 18:13-27).

- This style of leadership is pastor-led as opposed to congregation-led. However, the Moses Model should still have a board of elders who support the pastor spiritually through prayer, and physically by taking on some of the pastor's responsibilities by dividing the work load.

- Some people criticize the Moses Model because they say it lacks accountability because pastors can easily abuse their authority. Of course, anyone serving with wrong motives can abuse their position.

- As long as church leaders obey God's Word, this model of leadership is sound. The Bible says that church leaders should "*care for the flock that God has entrusted to you. Watch over it willingly, not grudgingly - not for what you will get out of it, but because you are eager to serve God. Don't lord it over the people assigned to your care, but lead them by your own good example. And when the Great Shepherd appears, you will receive a crown of never-ending glory and honor*" (1 Peter 5:2-4 NLT).

> **Philippians 1:2 (NASB).** ²Grace to you and peace from **God our Father** and the **Lord Jesus Christ**.

Commentary. Paul continued his greeting by wishing grace and peace to the believers in Philippi. We know from our study on Ephesians that grace means unmerited favor, and peace in Hebrew means shalom, which is a Jewish greeting meaning may health and prosperity be upon you.

Paul concluded his brief greeting by mentioning two members of the Trinity; God the Father and Jesus the Son. The doctrine of the Trinity can be found throughout the Bible, starting in Genesis where God said, "*Let Us make mankind in Our image, according to Our likeness*" (Genesis 1:26). The Gospel of Matthew also mentioned the three members of the Trinity when Jesus told His apostles to "*Go and make disciples of all the nations, baptizing them in the name of the Father and the Son and the Holy Spirit*" (Matthew 28:19). These verses clearly describe the plurality of God as three separate persons. The Trinity is a difficult concept to understand and the limits of the human mind make it impossible to fully comprehend an infinite God in three persons.

(Q) HOW WOULD YOU DESCRIBE THE TRINITY? _____

(Q) ANY COMMENTS ON THESES VERSES? _____

> **Stop and discuss the above comments and questions — Answer to questions are on the next page.**

> **Philippians 1:3-5 (NASB).** ³I thank my God in all my remembrance of you, ⁴always offering prayer with **joy** in my every prayer for you all, ⁵**in view of your participation in the gospel** from the first day until now.

Commentary. As we said in the introduction, Philippians has been called **Paul's joy letter** because it emphasizes the joy of the Christian life as well as Paul's gratitude for the believers in Philippi. Paul told them that he prays and thanks God for them all the time. He was expressing his joy for the Philippians faithfulness. It is the same joy that the Apostle John wrote about to Gaius when he said, "*I was overjoyed when brothers came and testified that you are walking in truth. I have no greater joy than this, to hear of my children walking in the truth*" (3 John 1:3-4).

Reflective Question: Are you happy when you see other ministries growing and bringing the lost into God's kingdom? Or are you jealous and secretly wish your ministry would outgrow theirs?

(Q) WHAT DOES VERSE 5 MEAN? _____

(Q) ANY COMMENTS ON THESES VERSES? _____

> **Stop and discuss the above comments and questions — Answer to questions are on the next page.**

Answers to Questions from the Previous Page

(Q) HOW WOULD YOU DESCRIBE THE TRINITY?

As we said earlier, it is impossible to describe an infinite God with a finite mind. However, there are several illustrations that people have used in trying to describe the Trinity. Here are three examples. Keep in mind, none of these examples are completely accurate.

- **Water** can be liquid, ice or steam. All of these consist of the same ingredients, H2O. Therefore, liquid, ice and steam are H2O in three forms.

- **An Egg** consists of a shell, a yoke and the white. Each are part of the egg, but not the egg itself.

- **An Apple** consists of the skin, flesh and seeds. Like the egg, each are part of the apple, but not the apple itself.

- Maybe your group came up with a better way to describe the Trinity.

(Q) WHAT DOES VERSE 5 MEAN?

> **Philippians 1:3-5 (NASB).** [3] I thank my God in all my remembrance of you, [4] always offering prayer with **joy** in my every prayer for you all, [5] **in view of your participation in the gospel** from the first day until now.

- The Message Bible says, "*For you have been my partners in spreading the Good News about Christ from the time you first heard it until now*" (Philippians 1:5 MSG).

- Paul visited Philippi ten years earlier during his second missionary journey. This means that Paul and the Philippians have been friends and partners in ministry for over ten years.

- Paul was acknowledging their longtime friendship and thanking them for their commitment and partnership in the spreading of the Gospel.

- When you or your church support a missionary through prayer, hospitality, and financially, you are also partnering with them in spreading the Gospel and would have the same relationship as Paul did with the Philippians.

Philippians 1:6 (NASB). [6] For I am confident of this very thing, that He who began a good work among you will complete it by the **day of Christ Jesus**.

Commentary. This verse starts with Paul saying "*I am confident of this very thing.*" What thing? He is confident that God will complete the good work He started in the lives of believers. The application of this verse is that Christ started a good work in each believer the moment they accepted Him as their Lord and Savior. This moment is called **justification** and begins the life-long process of **sanctification** where God molds and guides believers to be more like Christ. In other words, Christians can be sure that God will finish what He started by the time He returns for His church.

Reflective Question: Are you discouraged because you don't feel like you are making progress in your spiritual life? Have you forgotten that God has promised to finish the good work He started in you?

(Q) WHAT IS "*THE DAY OF CHRIST JESUS*"? _____

(Q) ANY COMMENTS ON THESES VERSES? _____

Stop and discuss the above comments and questions — Answer to questions are on the next page.

Philippians 1:7-8 (NASB). [7] For it is only right for me to feel this way about you all, because I **have you in my heart**, since both in my imprisonment and in the defense and confirmation of the gospel, you all are partakers of grace with me. [8] For God is my witness, **how I long for you** all with the affection of Christ Jesus.

Commentary. Can you hear Paul's heart? He misses his friends and longs to be with them. These verses clearly show that this epistle is different than Paul's other letters. The main difference is that this is a personal letter written to friends, rather than a formal letter written to correct the congregation. Paul loved the Philippians and they loved him. Jesus said, "*By this all people will know that you are My disciples: if you have love for one another*" (John 13:35). Love is the evidence of the Holy Spirit's presence in the life of the Christian.

Wayne Wiersbe said it this way, "*When we permit God to perform His 'good work' in us, then we grow in our love for one another.*" The Philippians were partners in ministry with Paul, and they loved him and financially supported his mission to spread the Gospel throughout the world.

Reflective Question: If you went to court and were charged with "loving others," would there be enough evidence to convict you?

(Q) WHAT IS THE "*EVIDENCE OF LOVE*" IN THE CHRISTIANS LIFE? _____

(Q) ANY COMMENTS ON THESES VERSES? _____

Stop and discuss the above comments and questions — Answer to questions are on the next page.

Answers to Questions from the Previous Page

Q) WHAT IS "*THE DAY OF CHRIST JESUS*"?

- This is a reference to the **Rapture** when Jesus returns for His church. Paul described this as **the day of Christ** in his first letter to the Thessalonians when he wrote: "*For the Lord Himself will descend from heaven with a shout, with the voice of the archangel and with the trumpet of God, and the dead in Christ will rise first. Then we who are alive, who remain, will be caught up together with them in the clouds to meet the Lord in the air, and so we will always be with the Lord*" (1 Thessalonians 4:16–17).

- The chart below shows the seven-year Tribulation period and the events that have been prophesized in the book of Daniel, Isaiah and Revelation. This is the **pre-trib** view of the Rapture.

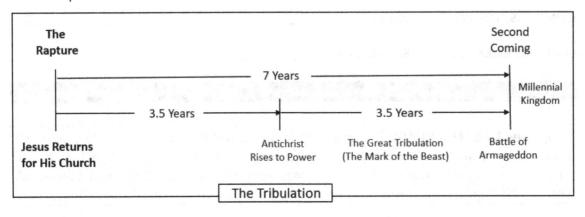

(Q) WHAT IS THE "*EVIDENCE OF LOVE*" IN THE CHRISTIANS LIFE?

- A good place to start is the love chapter from Paul's first letter to the Corinthians.

    "*Love is patient, love is kind, it is not jealous; love does not brag, it is not arrogant. It does not act disgracefully, it does not seek its own benefit; it is not provoked, does not keep an account of a wrong suffered, it does not rejoice in unrighteousness, but rejoices with the truth; it keeps every confidence, it believes all things, hopes all things, endures all things. Love never fails*" (1 Corinthians 13:4-8).

- Another place to look for evidence of love is the "*Fruit of the Spirit.*"

    "*But the fruit of the Spirit is love, joy, peace, patience, kindness, goodness, faithfulness, gentleness, self-control; against such things there is no law*" (Galatians 5:22-23).

- Believers who practice love will always have joy in their hearts just as Paul did.

> **Philippians 1:9-10a (NASB).** [9] And this **I pray,** that your **love may overflow** still more and more in real knowledge and all discernment, [10] so that you may discover the things that are excellent.

Commentary. These verses are the beginning of **Paul's intercessory prayer** for the Philippians. His prayer was a simple prayer asking for love to overflow in the church. Jesus said that love is the mark of a Christian (John 13:35). In Paul's first letter to Thessalonica, he said, "*may the Lord cause you to increase and overflow in love for one another, and for all people*" (1 Thessalonians 3:12).

Paul was praying for believers to love in knowledge and discernment. What does this mean? It means to love with knowledge not just emotions so that you can discern right from wrong. Otherwise, your emotions may cloud your judgement. The Bible says the heart is deceitful (Jeremiah 17:9) and out of it comes many evil thoughts (Mark 7:21-23). Without wisdom your emotions will toss you around like the wind (James 1:6). So what is the solution for loving with discernment? The psalmist said, "*Create in me a clean heart, O' God, and renew a steadfast spirit within me*" (Psalm 51:10).

Reflective Question: *Do my emotions toss me around like the wind?*

(Q) WHAT DOES "*INTERCESSORY PRAYER*" MEAN? _____

(Q) ANY COMMENTS ON THESES VERSES? _____

Stop and discuss the above comments and questions — Answer to questions are on the next page.

> **Philippians 1:10b-11 (NASB).** That you may be sincere and blameless for the **day of Christ**; [11] having been filled with the **fruit of righteousness** which comes through Jesus Christ, for the glory and praise of God.

Commentary. Paul continued his intercessory prayer for the Philippians to love with knowledge and discernment so they will be blameless on the day of Christ. The **day of Christ** is a reference to a future event called the Rapture. Do not confuse the day of Christ with the **day of the Lord**.

- **The day of Christ** is a time of joy where God returns for His people and will end the believers struggle against sin and death. It is also a time where God distributes the believer's inheritance.

- **The day of the Lord** is a time of judgement where God pours out His wrath on unrepentant sinners. The Bible says that on that day, the Lord "*will bring darkness, not light*" (Amos 5:18 NLT).

Paul's desire was for the believers in Philippi to show evidence of their righteousness which comes through the Holy Spirit working in and through them.

(Q) DOES BLAMELESS MEAN "*WITHOUT SIN*"? _____

(Q) ANY COMMENTS ON THESES VERSES? _____

Stop and discuss the above comments and questions — Answer to questions are on the next page.

Answers to Questions from the Previous Page

(Q) WHAT DOES "*INTERCESSORY PRAYER*" MEAN?

- Intercessory prayer is prayer that is offered up on behalf of another person.

- The Bible says that Jesus is the mediator between God and man, and because of this, all believers have the Holy Spirit and can intercede in prayer on behalf of other people (1 Timothy 2:5).

(Q) DOES BLAMELESS MEAN "*WITHOUT SIN*"?

- Before answering this question, let's look at a couple of definitions. The dictionary defines blameless as someone who is not responsible for a problem and is free from fault.

- The biblical definition is someone who cannot be accused of wrongdoing before people or God because they are innocent or above reproach.

- Now let's answer the question: "does blameless mean without sin"?

- The answer is no, no one has ever lived a sinless life except Jesus Christ.

- The key verse is the one that comes after blameless which says, "*having been filled with the fruit of righteousness which comes through Jesus Christ, for the glory and praise of God*" (Philippians 1:11).

- In other words, believers are seen as blameless before God because of the righteousness they received after placing their faith in Jesus Christ. They are still sinners but are seen as sinless because of the righteousness they received from Jesus when He paid their sin debt.

Let's RE-Read Tonight's Verses

Philippians 1:1-11 (NASB). [1] Paul and Timothy, bondservants of Christ Jesus,

~~~~~~

To all the saints in Christ Jesus who are in Philippi, including the overseers and deacons:

~~~~~~

[2] Grace to you and peace from God our Father and the Lord Jesus Christ.

~~~~~~

[3] I thank my God in all my remembrance of you, [4] always offering prayer with joy in my every prayer for you all, [5] in view of your participation in the gospel from the first day until now.

~~~~~~

[6] For I am confident of this very thing, that He who began a good work among you will complete it by the day of Christ Jesus.

~~~~~~

[7] For it is only right for me to feel this way about you all, because I have you in my heart,

~~~~~~

since both in my imprisonment and in the defense and confirmation of the gospel, you all are partakers of grace with me.

~~~~~~

[8] For God is my witness, how I long for you all with the affection of Christ Jesus.

~~~~~~

[9] And this I pray, that your love may overflow still more and more in real knowledge and all discernment,

~~~~~~

[10] so that you may discover the things that are excellent, that you may be sincere and blameless for the day of Christ;

~~~~~~

[11] having been filled with the fruit of righteousness which comes through Jesus Christ, for the glory and praise of God.

(Q) ANY FINAL COMMENTS? _____

This is the end of this week's study.

Philippians: Rejoice in the Lord

WEEK 2 - PHILIPPIANS 1:12-30

Let's Review Last Week's Study

The theme of this letter is joy and was co-written by the Apostle Paul and Timothy to the churches in Philippi about ten years after Paul's second missionary journey. In their introduction, Paul and Timothy described themselves as bondservants which means Doulos. A Doulos is "someone who belongs to another person and has no rights of their own." By describing themselves as bondservants of Christ, they were saying they have chosen to serve Jesus for the rest of their lives.

A key verse from last week's study is, "*He who began a good work among you will complete it by the day of Christ Jesus*" (Philippians 1:6). This verse is referring to two things: (1) the sanctification of the believer and (2) the day of Christ, also known as the Rapture which is when Jesus returns for His church. Sanctification is the life-long process where God molds and guides the believer to be more like Christ. Christians can be sure that God will keep His promise and finish what He started by the time He returns for His church.

Then Paul prayed for his friends and expressed how much he loved and missed them. He also prayed that their love would overflow with knowledge and discernment so that they would be clothed in righteousness and found blameless before God the Father (Philippians 1:9-11).

(Q) WHAT IS THE DIFFERENCE BETWEEN THE "*DAY OF CHRIST*" AND THE "*DAY OF THE LORD*"?
_____

(Q) ANY COMMENTS ON LAST WEEK'S STUDY? _____

Stop and discuss the above comments and questions — Answer to questions are on the next page.

Let's Review Tonight's Study

Tonight, we find Paul comforting the believers in Philippi because they are worried about him being in prison. He reassured them that his imprisonment was part of God's plan to bring salvation to Rome, and that most of the house of Nero have become Christians as the result of his detention.

A key verse from tonight's study is "*For to me, to live is Christ, and to die is gain*" (Philippians 1:21). How can dying be gain? We'll find the answer to this later tonight when we discuss this verse in context with the other verses. Another key verse from this chapter is Christians should "*conduct themselves in a manner worthy of the gospel of Christ*" by standing united in one spirit and one mind. (Philippians 1:27). Paul was addressing a disagreement between two women that caused a division in the church.

Paul ended this chapter with a warning to the believers that they will suffer persecution in the same way he has suffered (Philippians 1:30). The Bible has many verses cautioning believers about suffering for simply being a faithful follower of Christ. Likewise, the Bible also has many verses encouraging believers during times of persecution and trials.

(Q) WHAT CAN CHRISTIANS DO DURING TIMES OF TRIAL AND PERSECUTION?
_____

(Q) ANY COMMENTS ON THESES VERSES? _____

Stop and discuss the above comments and questions — Answer to questions are on the next page.

Answers to Questions from the Previous Page

(Q) WHAT IS THE DIFFERENCE BETWEEN THE "*DAY OF CHRIST*" AND THE "*DAY OF THE LORD*"?

- **The day of Christ** is a time of joy where God returns for His people and will end the believers struggle against sin and death. The day of Christ is also known as the Rapture which will begin the seven years of the Tribulation.

- **The day of the Lord** is a time of judgement where God pours out His wrath on unrepentant sinners. The Bible says, "*What sorrow awaits you who say, 'If only the day of the Lord were here.' You have no idea what you are wishing for. That day will bring darkness, not light*" (Amos 5:18 NLT).

(Q) WHAT CAN CHRISTIANS DO DURING TIMES OF TRIAL AND PERSECUTION?

- The first thing Christians can do is turn to God in prayer and ask for His protection and direction (1 John 5:14-15).

- Christians should lay their concerns and anxieties at the foot of the cross (1 Peter 5:7).

- Christians are commanded to pray for their persecutors and to not seek revenge (1 Thessalonians 5:15, Luke 23:34). However, Christians should flee to safety if their life is in danger (Acts 14:5-6).

- The Bible says that persecution and trials have value for believers. For example, the Apostle Pauls said *We celebrate in our tribulations, knowing that tribulations bring about perseverance; and perseverance, proven character; and proven character, hope; and hope does not disappoint (Romans 5:3-4).*

Let's Begin Tonight's Study

> **Philippians 1:12-14 (NASB).** [12] Now I want you to know, brothers and sisters, that **my circumstances** have turned out for the greater progress of the gospel, [13] so that **my imprisonment** in the cause of Christ has become well known throughout the praetorian guard and to everyone else, [14] and that most of the brothers and sisters, trusting in the Lord because of **my imprisonment**, have far more courage to speak the word of God without fear.

Commentary. The Philippians were distressed because their friend was unjustly imprisoned and there was the real possibility of him being executed. Paul tried to comfort them by saying his imprisonment was part of God's plan to bring salvation to Rome.

How did God use Paul's imprisonment to bring salvation to Rome? Paul was chained to a Roman guard day and night, and the guards were rotated every six hours. One by one, Paul was able to share the Gospel with every single Roman guard. The result was that God used Paul's circumstances to bring the good news to Rome, especially to the house of Nero. Think about that, all of Nero's soldiers became Christians!

(Q) HAVE YOU EVER BEEN THROUGH A DIFFICULT TRIAL WHERE GOD USED IT FOR HIS GLORY?

_____

(Q) ANY COMMENTS ON THESES VERSES? _____

> **Stop and discuss the above verses and questions — Answer to questions are on the next page.**

> **Philippians 1:15-18 (NASB).** [15] Some, to be sure, are preaching Christ even from **envy and strife**, but some also from goodwill; [16] the latter do it out of love, knowing that I am appointed for the defense of the gospel; [17] the former proclaim Christ out of **selfish ambition** rather than from pure motives, thinking that they are causing me distress in my imprisonment. [18] What then? Only that in every way, whether in pretense or in truth, Christ is proclaimed, and in this I rejoice.

Commentary. Paul was a strong leader and he had many friends, but he also had many enemies. In these verses Paul mentioned his friends in ministry who were preaching the Gospel out of love for God and pure motives. Then Paul mentioned those who opposed him that were preaching the Gospel out of selfish ambition and jealousy. They considered Paul their rival and their motives were to make Paul look bad while he was in prison.

Isn't it still like that today? Some believers are threatened by the success of other Christians and see them as the enemy rather than partners in ministry. These people serve with wrong motives because their real desire is to receive praise and honor from men rather than to please the Lord (Matthew 6:3-4).

(Q) WHY WASN'T PAUL BOTHERED THAT SOME BELIEVERS WERE PREACHING WITH BAD MOTIVES?

_____

(Q) ANY COMMENTS ON THESES VERSES? _____

> **Stop and discuss the above verses and questions — Answer to questions are on the next page.**

Answers to Questions from the Previous Page

(Q) HAVE YOU EVER BEEN THROUGH A DIFFICULT TRIAL WHERE GOD USED IT FOR HIS GLORY?

- Testimony time.
- Ask one or two people to share a trial where God used it for His glory.
- This is not a full-blown testimony. Keep the sharing to about two minutes each.

(Q) WHY WASN'T PAUL BOTHERED THAT SOME BELIEVERS WERE PREACHING WITH BAD MOTIVES?

- The answer is in verse 18, where Paul said "*Christ is proclaimed, and in this I rejoice.*"
- The Message Bible says it this way, "*I've decided that I really don't care about their motives, whether mixed, bad, or indifferent. Every time one of them opens his mouth, Christ is proclaimed, so I just cheer them on*" (Philippians 1:18 MSG).
- Paul didn't care about himself or his reputation. What he cared about was the Gospel was being preached and people were being saved. This is a lesson we can apply to our lives today.

> **Philippians 1:19-20 (NASB).** But not only that, I also will rejoice, ¹⁹ **for I know that this will turn out for my deliverance** through your prayers and the provision of the Spirit of Jesus Christ, ²⁰ according to my eager **expectation and hope,** that I will not be put to shame in anything, but that with all boldness, Christ will even now, as always, be exalted in my body, whether by life or by death.

Commentary. After Paul finished discussing the two groups who were preaching the Gospel, he brought the conversation back to his imprisonment. He said his imprisonment didn't shut him up, but it gave him a platform to make Christ more known (Philippians 1:20 MSG). It's clear from verse 19 that Paul expected to be released from prison. Why wouldn't he expect to be released? The Holy Spirit had already freed him once during his first trip to Philippi (Acts 16:26). And now Paul expected to be freed again through "*the provision of the Spirit of Jesus Christ.*" His faith and dependence on the Lord were strong and he believed that if God wanted to deliver him, then God would free him. Nevertheless, Paul had several concerns that he expressed in verse 20.

(Q) WHAT WERE PAUL'S THREE CONCERNS? _____

(Q) ANY COMMENTS ON THESES VERSES? _____

Stop and discuss the above verses and questions — Answer to questions are on the next page.

> **Philippians 1:21-22 (NASB).** ²¹ **For to me, to live is Christ, and to die is gain**. ²² But if I am to live on in the flesh, this will mean fruitful labor for me; and I do not know which to choose.

Commentary. Paul was having an internal battle between living and dying. If he was convicted, he would be put to death and be instantly in the presence of the Lord. How wonderful would that be? Plus his death might cause the gospel message to spread even faster because it has been said that, "*The blood of martyrs is like the seed of the church*" (Tertullian). On the other hand, if Paul were acquitted, he would be freed to continue preaching the good news and bringing more people to the Lord. However, it also meant that he would experience more beatings and persecution.

Paul had a passion for leading people to the Lord. How about you? Do you have the same passion and urgency that Paul had for sharing the good news? Or are you afraid to share the Gospel because you'll be rejected. Or maybe you tell yourself, "I'll share the good news tomorrow." This is one of Satan's biggest tricks; convincing believers they have plenty of time to share the good news, just not today.

Reflective Question: *What will your legacy be after you die? How will people remember you?*

(Q) WHY WAS PAUL STRUGGLING WITH LIVING OR DYING? _____

(Q) ANY COMMENTS ON THESES VERSES? _____

Stop and discuss the above verses and questions — Answer to questions are on the next page.

Answers to Questions from the Previous Page

(Q) WHAT WERE PAUL'S THREE CONCERNS?

- It might be easier to answer this question by looking at a different Bible translation. The New Living Translation says, *"For I fully expect and hope that **I will never be ashamed**, but that **I will continue to be bold for Christ**, as I have been in the past. And I trust that **my life will bring honor to Christ**, whether I live or die"* (Philippians 1:20 NLT).

- Therefore, Paul's three concerns were:

  1. He would never be ashamed of his faith in Christ.

  2. He would continue to boldly preach the Gospel.

  3. His life would bring honor to God.

- These are good goals for all believers.

(Q) WHY WAS PAUL STRUGGLING WITH LIVING OR DYING?

- Paul was in prison because he was falsely accused of crimes he did not commit, and he had been beaten several times were he almost died. So, his desire was to die and be in the presence of the Lord and not be in pain anymore.

- However, he recognized that he still had work to do for the Lord and that was to continue to share the good news and bring people to Christ. Plus, if he died the Philippians would lose a great friend, teacher and pastor.

- So his struggle was to do what was best for himself or do what was best for other people.

- The Message Bible says it this way, *"As long as I'm alive in this body, there is good work for me to do. If I had to choose right now, I hardly know which I'd choose. Hard choice! The desire to break camp here and be with Christ is powerful. Some days I can think of nothing better. But most days, because of what you are going through, I am sure that it's better for me to stick it out here"* (Philippians 1:22-24 MSG).

> **Philippians 1:23-24 (NASB).** ²³ But I am hard-pressed from both directions, having the desire to depart and be with Christ, for that is very much better; ²⁴ **yet to remain on in the flesh is more necessary for your sakes**.

Commentary. Paul's life mission was to serve the Lord and bring sinners to Christ. His passion was so strong that he told the Roman Christians he was willing to go to hell if he thought it would save the Israelites (Romans 9:1-3). *Wow, think about that.* Would you give up your place in heaven to save your family or friends from the gates of hell?

Despite Paul's passion for the lost, he had another desire that was even stronger and that was to be with Jesus in heaven. This created a dilemma for Paul; do what was best for himself or do what was best for other people. Paul knew the answer was to "*remain in the flesh*" and continue planting churches and discipling young believers.

At this point, Paul had been in the mission field for over twenty years and during this time, he had been harassed, beaten and wrongly imprisoned many times. It's not a stretch to say that Paul may have been tired and dejected. Believers today need to be careful not to take on too much ministry work or they may get burned out. Burnout happens when a person is so tired they lose interest in ministry work and it can lead to health issues such as depression or worse.

(Q) WHAT CAN BELIEVERS DO IF THEY ARE FEELING BURNED OUT FROM MINISTRY WORK? _____
_____

(Q) ANY COMMENTS ON THESES VERSES? _____

> **Stop and discuss the above verses and questions — Answer to questions are on the next page.**

> **Philippians 1:25-26 (NASB).** ²⁵ Convinced of this, I know that I will remain and continue with you all for your progress and joy in the faith, ²⁶ so that your pride in Christ Jesus may be abundant because of me by my coming to you again.

Commentary. In the previous verses Paul mentioned the possibility of being put to death or being released from prison. Now he was saying he was sure that he would be released and that when he was freed he would visit the Philippians again.

The NLT Bible says it this way, "*I am convinced that I will remain alive so I can continue to help all of you grow and experience the joy of your faith. And when I come to you again, you will have even more reason to take pride in Christ Jesus because of what He is doing through me*" (Philippians 1:25-26 NLT). Even after being wrongly imprisoned, Paul was full of joy and his faith remained steadfast and strong.

(Q) WHAT DOES VERSE 26 MEAN? _____

(Q) ANY COMMENTS ON THESES VERSES? _____

> **Stop and discuss the above verses and questions — Answer to questions are on the next page.**

Answers to Questions from the Previous Page

(Q) WHAT CAN BELIEVERS DO IF THEY ARE FEELING BURNED OUT FROM MINISTRY WORK?

- Let's look at a couple of examples in the Bible where people were experiencing burnout.
  - The apostles in the early church were heading for burnout until they delegated the work load to seven men of good reputation (Acts 6:1-6).
  - Moses was heading for burnout until his father-in-law advised him to divide the work load among the people (Exodus 18:14-23).
- Burnout is often the result of relying on self instead of trusting and relying on God. Here are some suggestions:
  - Learn to say "no" and set healthy boundaries. This may be difficult at first because people might be used to you taking on work even when they know you have a full plate.
  - Learn to accept help from other people. God gave each believer spiritual gifts so that the body of Christ can share in the work of the ministry (Romans 12:6-8).
  - Be intentional with your time. Avoid making quick decisions when approached to take on more ministry work.
  - Learn how to laugh and have fun again. Exercise and/or find a hobby, and remember to get proper rest and sleep (Hebrews 4:9-11).
  - Work for the Lord not for man's approval (Colossians 3:23).
- One of the tricks of the enemy is to keep Christians so busy doing things that their relationship with God gets put on the back burner.
- Take time to be with the Lord through prayer and meditation.

(Q) WHAT DOES VERSE 26 MEAN?

> **Philippians 1:26 (NASB).** [26] When I come to you again, you will have even more reason to **take pride in Christ Jesus** because of what **He is doing through me**

- Paul was simply saying that his friendship with the Philippians was special and that if he was able to visit Philippi again, they would be happy to see him and hear of the amazing things that God was doing through him.

> **Philippians 1:27-28 (NASB).** [27] **Only conduct yourselves in a manner worthy of the gospel of Christ**, so that whether I come and see you or remain absent, I will hear about you that you are standing firm in one spirit, with one mind striving together for the faith of the gospel; [28] and in no way alarmed by your opponents—which is a sign of destruction for them, but of salvation for you, and this too from God.

Commentary. It has been said "the greatest Gospel is your life." Why is that? It is because nonbelievers and believers are watching and scrutinizing your behavior all the time (Hebrews 12:1). In verse 27, Paul was encouraging the Philippians to conduct themselves in *"a manner worthy of the gospel of Christ"* and to stand united in one spirit and one mind.

Paul's call for unity was to address a conflict between two women that were threatening to divide the church. We'll discuss this conflict later in chapter 4. He also wanted the Philippians to know that he was getting reports about their progress and hoped to visit them after he was released from prison.

Reflective Question: Are you conducting yourself in a manner worthy of the Gospel of Christ?

(Q) WHAT DOES VERSE 28 MEAN? _____

(Q) ANY COMMENTS ON THESES VERSES? _____

Stop and discuss the above verses and questions — Answer to questions are on the next page.

> **Philippians 1:29-30 (NASB).** [29] For to you it has been granted for Christ's sake, not only to believe in Him, but also to **suffer on His behalf**, [30] **experiencing the same conflict which you saw in me**, and now hear to be in me.

Commentary. In these verses, Paul told the believers they have been *"granted"* the honor of suffering with Christ for their belief in Jesus. This must have come as a shock to the Philippians to hear they would suffer for their faith in the same way Paul has suffered. By saying they have been granted suffering on Jesus's behalf, Paul was letting the Philippians know they were **not** being punished by God and that it was an honor to suffer along with Christ.

Christians today will also suffer persecution for their faith, but their suffering will not be in vain. Listen to the Apostle Peter: *"If you suffer for doing what is right, God will reward you for it"* (1 Peter 3:14 NLT). The Apostle James also encouraged believers to persevere through trials so they can receive the crown of life reserved for those who love God (James 1:12). The Bible has many more verses describing the **cost** for following Jesus as well as the **benefits** for suffering for their faith.

(Q) HOW COME SOME BELIEVERS DO NOT UNDERSTAND THE COST FOR FOLLOWING JESUS? ____
_____

(Q) ANY COMMENTS ON THESES VERSES? _____

Stop and discuss the above verses and questions — Answer to questions are on the next page.

Answers to Questions from the Previous Page

(Q) WHAT DOES VERSE 28 MEAN?

> **Philippians 1:28 (NASB).** [28] In no way [be] alarmed by your opponents—which is a sign of destruction for them, but of salvation for you, and this too from God.

- Who were their opponents? Their opponents or adversaries were nonbelievers under the control and direction of Satan. These are the same adversaries facing Christians today.

- When believers **stand up** against their opponent, it shows the enemies of God that their destruction is certain.

- When believers are **not afraid** of their opponents, it shows the enemies of God the confidence that believers have in their God and their salvation.

- When the enemies of God fail to make believers afraid, they have failed because they have no other weapons beside fear and intimidation.

(Q) HOW COME SOME BELIEVERS DO NOT UNDERSTAND THE COST FOR FOLLOWING JESUS?

There are many reasons for this, here are just a couple.

1. They are a new believer who has not read through the Bible yet.

2. They have been a Christian for a while but are still immature in their faith, or they have never been discipled by a mature believer.

What is the cost for following Jesus?

- Jesus said to His disciples, *"If anyone wants to come after Me, he must deny himself, take up his cross, and follow Me. For whoever wants to save his life will lose it; but whoever loses his life for My sake will find it."* (Matthew 16:24-25).

- The Bible has a warning for people who do not read and study God's Word. It says, *"They hear the message and immediately receive it with joy. But since they don't have deep roots, they don't last long. They fall away as soon as they have problems or are persecuted for believing God's Word"* (Mark 4:16-17 MSG).

- Now that you know the cost, are you willing to pay the price for following Jesus?

Let's RE-Read Tonight's Verses

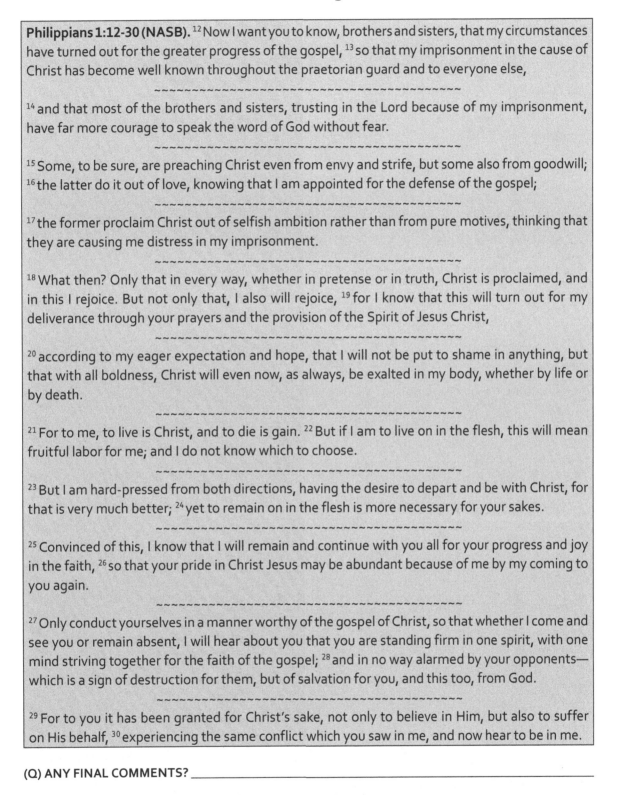

Philippians 1:12-30 (NASB). ¹²Now I want you to know, brothers and sisters, that my circumstances have turned out for the greater progress of the gospel, ¹³so that my imprisonment in the cause of Christ has become well known throughout the praetorian guard and to everyone else,

~~~~~~

¹⁴and that most of the brothers and sisters, trusting in the Lord because of my imprisonment, have far more courage to speak the word of God without fear.

~~~~~~

¹⁵Some, to be sure, are preaching Christ even from envy and strife, but some also from goodwill; ¹⁶the latter do it out of love, knowing that I am appointed for the defense of the gospel;

~~~~~~

¹⁷the former proclaim Christ out of selfish ambition rather than from pure motives, thinking that they are causing me distress in my imprisonment.

~~~~~~

¹⁸What then? Only that in every way, whether in pretense or in truth, Christ is proclaimed, and in this I rejoice. But not only that, I also will rejoice, ¹⁹for I know that this will turn out for my deliverance through your prayers and the provision of the Spirit of Jesus Christ,

~~~~~~

²⁰according to my eager expectation and hope, that I will not be put to shame in anything, but that with all boldness, Christ will even now, as always, be exalted in my body, whether by life or by death.

~~~~~~

²¹For to me, to live is Christ, and to die is gain. ²²But if I am to live on in the flesh, this will mean fruitful labor for me; and I do not know which to choose.

~~~~~~

²³But I am hard-pressed from both directions, having the desire to depart and be with Christ, for that is very much better; ²⁴yet to remain on in the flesh is more necessary for your sakes.

~~~~~~

²⁵Convinced of this, I know that I will remain and continue with you all for your progress and joy in the faith, ²⁶so that your pride in Christ Jesus may be abundant because of me by my coming to you again.

~~~~~~

²⁷Only conduct yourselves in a manner worthy of the gospel of Christ, so that whether I come and see you or remain absent, I will hear about you that you are standing firm in one spirit, with one mind striving together for the faith of the gospel; ²⁸and in no way alarmed by your opponents—which is a sign of destruction for them, but of salvation for you, and this too, from God.

~~~~~~

²⁹For to you it has been granted for Christ's sake, not only to believe in Him, but also to suffer on His behalf, ³⁰experiencing the same conflict which you saw in me, and now hear to be in me.

(Q) ANY FINAL COMMENTS? _____

This is the end of this week's study.

Notes

40

Philippians:
Rejoice in the Lord

WEEK 3 - PHILIPPIANS 2:1-16

Let's Review Last Week's Study

Paul comforted the believers because they were worried about him in prison. He reassured them that his imprisonment was part of God's plan to bring salvation to Rome. By this time, Paul had completed three missionary journeys and was away from Philippi for over ten years. During his three missionary journeys he was harassed, beaten and wrongly imprisoned. It is reasonable to think that Paul was feeling burned out when he said, "*For to me, to live is Christ, and to die is gain*" (Philippians 1:21).

Paul was having an internal battle between living and dying. On the one hand, if he was convicted of a crime, he would be put to death, and instantly be in the presence of the Lord. On the other hand, if Paul was acquitted, he would be able to continue preaching the good news and bringing people to the Lord. However, it also meant that he would face more persecution and beatings.

Then Paul addressed an issue that was threatening to divide the church. He encouraged the believers to "*conduct themselves in a manner worthy of the gospel of Christ*" so that they would remain united in one spirit and one mind. (Philippians 1:27).

Paul ended chapter one with a warning to the believers that they will suffer persecution in the same way he has suffered. The Bible has many verses cautioning believers about suffering for simply being a faithful follower of Christ.

(Q) WHAT CAN BELIEVERS DO IF THEY ARE FEELING BURNED OUT FROM MINISTRY WORK?

_____

(Q) ANY COMMENTS ON LAST WEEK'S STUDY? _____

Stop and discuss the above comments and questions — Answer to questions are on the next page.

Let's Review Tonight's Study

Paul began this chapter by continuing his discussion on the conflict that was threatening to divide the church. He cautioned the Christians who were serving in the church to have a *self-less* attitude, rather than *self-ish* motives. Paul encouraged the believers to "*have the same attitude that Christ Jesus had*" (Philippians 2:6). Then Paul quoted Isaiah 45:23 as a warning to remind the Philippians that everyone will give an account of their lives at the **Bema Seat of Christ**.

The key verses for tonight are, "*Do all things without complaining or arguments; so that you will prove yourselves to be blameless and innocent, children of God above reproach in the midst of a crooked and perverse generation, among whom you appear as lights in the world*" (Philippians 2:14-15).

(Q) WHAT IS THE "*BEMA SEAT OF CHRIST*"? _____

(Q) ANY COMMENTS? _____

Stop and discuss the above comments and questions — Answer to questions are on the next page.

Answers to Questions from the Previous Page

(Q) WHAT CAN BELIEVERS DO IF THEY ARE FEELING BURNED OUT FROM MINISTRY WORK?

- Let's look at a couple of examples in the Bible where people were experiencing burnout.
  - o The apostles in the early church were heading for burnout until they delegated the work load to seven men of good reputation (Acts 6:1-6).
  - o Moses was heading for burnout until his father-in-law advised him to divide the work load among the people (Exodus 18:14-23).
- Burnout is often the result of relying on self instead of trusting and relying on God. Here are some suggestions:
  - o Learn to say "no" and set healthy boundaries. This may be difficult at first because people might be used to you taking on work even when they know you have a full plate.
  - o Learn to accept help from other people. God gave each believer spiritual gifts so that the body of Christ can share in the work of the ministry (Romans 12:6-8).
  - o Be intentional with your time. Avoid making quick decisions when approached to take on more ministry work.
  - o Learn how to laugh and have fun again. Exercise and/or find a hobby, and remember to get proper rest and sleep (Hebrews 4:9-11).
  - o Work for the Lord not for man's approval (Colossians 3:23).
- One of the tricks of the enemy is to keep Christians so busy doing things that their relationship with God gets put on the back burner.
- Take time to be with the Lord through prayer and meditation.

(Q) WHAT IS THE "*BEMA SEAT OF CHRIST*"?

- The "*Bema Seat of Christ*" is a judgment that will occur **after** God determines who is going to heaven and who is condemned to hell. This determination is based on who repented and followed Jesus, verses who denied Jesus.
- The "*Bema Seat of Christ*" is also called the "*Judgment Seat of Christ,*" and is where all Christians will give an account of themselves for the way they lived their lives. This judgment is for believers only. Nonbelievers will be judged at the "*Great White Throne Judgment*" (Revelation 20:11-15).
- Paul wrote about the Bema Seat of Christ in his second letter to the Corinthians when he said: "*For we must all appear before the **Judgment Seat of Christ**, so that each one may receive compensation for his deeds done through the body, in accordance with what he has done, whether good or bad*" (2 Corinthians 5:10).

Let's Begin Tonight's Study

> **Philippians 2:1-2 (NASB).** [1] Therefore **if** there is any encouragement in Christ, **if** any consolation of love, **if** any fellowship of the Spirit, **if** any affection and compassion, [2] **[then]** make my joy complete by being of the same mind, maintaining the same love, united in spirit, intent on one purpose.

Commentary. Paul began this chapter by addressing a conflict between two women. Their bickering was threatening to divide the church (Philippians 4:2-3). Paul reminded the Philippians of the love they have for one another through Christ. He did this in the form of an if-then statement.

If you have received encouragement, love, fellowship, affection and compassion,
Then make me happy and quit bickering and arguing with each other.

Reflective Question: Am I encouraging unity in my church family or am I sowing cords of discourse?

(Q) *"FELLOWSHIP IN THE SPIRIT"* IS ALSO CALLED *"KONONIA."* WHAT DOES KONONIA MEAN?
_____

(Q) ANY COMMENTS ON THESES VERSES? _____

> **Stop and discuss the above verses and questions — Answer to questions are on the next page.**

> **Philippians 2:3-4 (NASB).** [3] Do nothing from **selfishness** or **empty conceit**, but with humility consider one another as more important than yourselves; [4] do not merely look out for your own personal interests, but also for the interests of others.

Commentary. In verse 3, Paul was questioning the believer's motives for serving God. He was telling them, do not serve God to satisfy your own self-interest and self-importance. The Christians motive for serving should be to bring honor to God and not to themselves, or as Jesus said, if you want to be great in God's kingdom, then you must first be a servant (Matthew 20:26-28). In verse 4, Paul continued his rebuke of the Philippians by reminding them to be concerned for the needs of others. This does not mean they should neglect their own needs or the needs of their families.

Paul's words are timeless and still apply today. When you help others do not go around boasting of how much you gave or who you helped. In other words, don't help others just so you can be praised by people. Jesus said, *"When you give to the poor, do not let your left hand know what your right hand is doing, so that your charitable giving will be in secret; and your Father who sees what is done in secret will reward you"* (Matthew 6:2-4).

Reflective Question: Are you so self-absorbed that you don't have time to help other people?

(Q) WHAT IS THE DIFFERENCE BETWEEN *"SELF-IMPORTANCE"* AND *"SELF-ESTEEM"*? _____
_____

(Q) ANY COMMENTS ON THESES VERSES? _____

> **Stop and discuss the above verses and questions — Answer to questions are on the next page.**

Answers to Questions from the Previous Page

(Q) *"FELLOWSHIP IN THE SPIRIT"* IS ALSO CALLED *"KONONIA."* WHAT DOES KONONIA MEAN?

- It means communion with God and with other believers. It is an intimate relationship with God that brings believers together as one "in Christ" and does away with the differences that divide.

- The early Christians *"continuously devoted themselves to [kononia]"* (Acts 2:42).

- The Apostle John said, *"if we walk in the Light as He Himself is in the Light, we have [kononia] with one another, and the blood of Jesus His Son cleanses us from all sin"* (1 John 1:7).

(Q) WHAT IS THE DIFFERENCE BETWEEN *"SELF-IMPORTANCE"* AND *"SELF-ESTEEM"*?

Self-Importance

- It is a preoccupation with oneself that is rooted in pride.

- Paul warned the Galatians about being preoccupied with self when he said, *"What a person plants, he will harvest. The person who plants selfishness, ignoring the needs of others, ignoring God, will harvest a crop of weeds. All he'll have to show for his life is weeds"* (Galatians 6:8 MSG).

Self-Esteem

- Healthy self-esteem is having an accurate and balanced view of one's own abilities that is not inflated.

- Healthy self-esteem comes from knowing your valuable because of the price that Jesus paid for you when He died on the cross.

- Healthy self-esteem comes from having a right relationship with God and staying away from sin that will enslave you.

- Unhealthy self-esteem comes from being so independent and prideful that you go right back into self-importance and an exaggerated view of oneself.

> **Philippians 2:5-8 (NASB).** [5] Have this attitude in yourselves which was also in Christ Jesus, [6] who, as He already existed in the form of God, did not consider equality with God something to be grasped, [7] but emptied Himself by taking the form of a **bond-servant** and being born in the likeness of men. [8] And being found in appearance as a man, He **humbled Himself** by becoming **obedient** to the point of death: death on a cross.

Commentary. In these verses, Paul makes a shift from calling for unity in the church to giving a theology lesson on the nature and identity of Christ. The NLT Bible says it this way, "*You must have the same attitude that Christ Jesus had*" (Philippians 2:6 NLT).

What does it mean to have the same attitude as Christ? The word attitude describes a person's views or feelings towards something or someone and can be positive or negative. For example, a person with a positive attitude might be called an optimist, and a person with a negative attitude might be called a pessimist. So how does this relate to Paul urging Christians to have the same attitude as Christ?

(Q) WHAT DOES IT MEAN TO HAVE THE "*SAME ATTITUDE AS CHRIST*"? _____

(Q) ANY COMMENTS ON THESES VERSES? _____

> **Stop and discuss the above verses and questions — Answer to questions are on the next page.**

> **Philippians 2:9-11 (NASB).** [9] For this reason also God highly exalted Him, and bestowed on Him **the name which is above every name,** [10] so that at the name of Jesus every knee will bow, of those who are in heaven and on earth and under the earth, [11] and that every tongue will confess that Jesus Christ is **Lord,** to the glory of God the Father.

Commentary. God raised Jesus from the dead to be with Him in the highest place of honor at His right hand. The expression "*higher than any other name*" means **Lord.** Jesus is Lord over all in heaven, on earth and under the earth. "*In heaven*" refers to all of the angels, including the fallen angels. "*On earth*" refers to people who are still alive, and "*under the earth*" refers to people who are in Sheol and have passed away and awaiting their judgment which is called the **Great White Throne Judgment**.

Verse 10 is a quote from Isaiah 45:23 that says "*every knee will bow and every tongue will confess that Jesus is Lord.*" On that day, believers and nonbelievers will bow down before God and ALL will know that Jesus is Lord. The Bible mentions several judgments. Let's discuss two of these judgments.

(Q) WHAT IS THE DIFFERENCE BETWEEN THE "*JUDGMENT SEAT OF CHRIST*" AND THE "*GREAT WHITE THRONE JUDGMENT*"? _____

(Q) ANY COMMENTS ON THESES VERSES? _____

> **Stop and discuss the above verses and questions — Answer to questions are on the next page.**

Answers to Questions from the Previous Page

(Q) WHAT DOES IT MEAN TO HAVE THE *"SAME ATTITUDE AS CHRIST"*?

> **Philippians 2:5-8 (NLT).** [5] You must have the same attitude that Christ Jesus had. [6] Though He was God, He did not think of equality with God as something to cling to. [7] Instead, He gave up His divine privileges; He took the **humble position** of a **slave** and was born as a human being. When He appeared in human form, [8] He humbled Himself in **obedience** to God and **died a criminal's death on a cross**.

- According to Paul, what was Jesus's attitude?
  - Even though He was God, He had a **humble** heart.
  - He willingly set aside His deity to become a **bondservant**.
  - He **obeyed God** the Father unto death.
  - He **sacrificed His life** by coming to earth as a man, where He was crucified and died a terrible death, all for the forgiveness of sin.
- Jesus's attitude was humility, obedience, servanthood and sacrifice for others.
- The application for today is that believers should have the same attitude as Jesus and should consider it a privilege to serve others.

(Q) WHAT IS THE DIFFERENCE BETWEEN THE *"JUDGMENT SEAT OF CHRIST"* AND THE *"GREAT WHITE THRONE JUDGMENT"*?

The Judgment Seat of Christ.

- This judgment is reserved for **believers** whose names are found in the book of life.
- This judgment is also called the "Bema Seat of Christ."
- This judgment is when Christians will give an account of themselves to God and be judged and rewarded for their deeds and service to God (Romans 14:12).

The Great White Throne Judgment.

- This judgment is reserved for **nonbelievers** and unrepentant sinners.
- This is the final judgment for nonbelievers before they are thrown into the lake of fire (Revelation 20:11-15, Daniel 12:1-2).

> **Philippians 2:12 (NASB).** [12] So then, my beloved, just as you have always obeyed, not as in my presence only, but now much more in my absence, **work out your own salvation with fear and trembling**.

Commentary. Paul was encouraging the Philippians to continue to **obey the Lord in his absence**. This fits in perfectly with the definition of integrity. Integrity means doing the right thing even when no one is watching, or in this case, even when Paul was in prison and couldn't be with them.

Then Paul said something interesting and a bit confusing. He said Christians should *"work out their own salvation with fear and trembling."* Does this sound like a works-based salvation? If that's what Paul meant to say, then this is in direct conflict with the Bible which says that salvation is faith in Jesus and nothing else!

Reflective Question: Do I do the right thing even when no one is watching? Or do I think I'm "getting away with sin" because no one saw me?

(Q) WHAT DID PAUL MEAN WHEN HE SAID *"WORK OUT YOUR SALVATION"*? _____

_____

(Q) ANY COMMENTS ON THESES VERSES? _____

Stop and discuss the above verses and questions — Answer to questions are on the next page.

> **Philippians 2:13 (NASB).** [13] For it is God who is at work **in you,** both to desire and to work for His good pleasure.

Commentary. This verse clarifies the reason for Christians to work out their salvation. The reason is because God is working in them. God does this because it pleases Him to work in each believer's life. There might be some lazy Christians who read this verse and think, "Hmmm, since God is working in me, then I don't need to do anything." Then they'll point to this verse as an excuse for their inaction.

Jesus told a story called the **Parable of the Talents** where a master entrusted talents to three stewards. To one he gave five talents, to another, two, and to another, one. When the master returned from his long journey, he called the three stewards in to settle their accounts. The two stewards who were given five and two talents doubled their talents. The master responded, *"Well done, good and faithful servant"* (Matthew 25:23). However, the steward who was given one talent did not earn any profit because he buried his talent. The master responded by calling him worthless and lazy for not investing the talent, and then the master took the stewards talent and ordered him thrown into that place where there is weeping and gnashing of teeth (Matthew 25:28-29).

(Q) WHAT IS THE MORAL OF THE *"PARABLE OF THE TALENTS"*? _____

(Q) ANY COMMENTS ON THESES VERSES? _____

Stop and discuss the above verses and questions — Answer to questions are on the next page.

Answers to Questions from the Previous Page

(Q) WHAT DID PAUL MEAN WHEN HE SAID "*WORK OUT YOUR SALVATION*"?

- Paul was encouraging the Philippians to put real effort into their Christian walk. He did not mean for them to work FOR their salvation, but rather to work OUT their salvation. By working out their salvation, they will be leaving evidence of their faith in every area of their life.

- Charles Spurgeon described this verse by telling this story; "*Some professors appear to have imbibed the notion that the grace of God is a kind of opium with which men may drug themselves into slumber, and their passion for strong doses of sleepy doctrine grows with that which it feeds on. 'God works in us,' say they, 'therefore there is nothing for us to do.' [This is] bad reasoning, [and a] false conclusion. God works, says the text; therefore we must work **out**, because God works **in***" (Charles Spurgeon).

(Q) WHAT IS THE MORAL OF THE "*PARABLE OF THE TALENTS*"?

- The two profitable stewards were praised and given increased responsibilities, and invited to enter into the joy of the Lord.

- The untrusting steward was scolded, rejected, and punished.

- The application of the parable as it relates to Philippians 2:13 is that God is working in the believer's life, but the believer must also work by using or investing the spiritual gifts he or she has been given to further the kingdom of God. Christians are accountable to God for the use of His resources and will give an account on judgement day.

- The question you must ask your self is: "Am I using the talents that God gave me for His kingdom?"

> **Philippians 2:14-15 (NASB).** [14] Do all things without complaining or arguments; [15] so that you will prove yourselves to be **blameless** and innocent, children of God **above reproach** in the midst of a crooked and perverse generation, among whom you appear as **lights in the world**.

Commentary. Paul was still addressing the conflict between two women that was threatening to divide the church. The Bible does not say what the conflict was about. However, we do know that a person with a critical spirit is discontent with their life, and a believer who constantly complains and gossips will lead to envy and strife with others. A Christian with this type of attitude will damage their opportunity to witness to nonbelievers. After all, who would be attracted to a church where its members are always complaining and arguing with each other? Nobody, that's who!

When believers keep their eyes on God, they prove themselves to be blameless and above reproach. But when they take their eyes off of God, they will sink like Peter did when he walked on water and took his eyes off of Jesus. Paul's words to the Philippians also applies to believers today. Christians are called to be the light in a crooked and perverse world. As the psalmist said, *"How wonderful and pleasant it is when brothers live together in harmony"* (Psalm 133:1 NLT).

Reflective Question: Do I have a critical spirit, or am I a Barnabas who encourages those around me?

(Q) WHAT DOES IT MEAN TO BE *"THE LIGHT OF THE WORLD"*? _____

(Q) ANY COMMENTS ON THESES VERSES? _____

Stop and discuss the above verses and questions — Answer to questions are on the next page.

> **Philippians 2:16 (NASB).** [16] Hold firmly [to] the **word of life**, so that on the **day of Christ** I can take pride because I did not run in vain nor labor in vain.

Commentary. In the previous verses Paul was describing the problems that occur when believers take their eyes off of Jesus and start relying on themselves. They move from the righteousness of God to self-righteousness or self-reliance. Now in this verse Paul encouraged the Philippians to stop arguing with each other and hold onto the *"word of life"*, which is Jesus. Paul was talking to the believers as their pastor, and his desire was for his flock to walk with the Lord, and he wanted to know that his efforts to disciple the Philippians was fruitful.

Have you ever discipled someone, where you poured yourself into them? Didn't it bring you joy to watch them grow in the Lord? Didn't it break your heart when they stumbled? That's how Paul felt. He loved the Philippians and he celebrated their faithfulness, and he mourned when they fell.

(Q) WHAT IS *"THE DAY OF CHRIST"*? _____

(Q) ANY COMMENTS ON THESES VERSES? _____

Stop and discuss the above verses and questions — Answer to questions are on the next page.

Answers to Questions from the Previous Page

(Q) WHAT DOES IT MEAN TO BE *"THE LIGHT OF THE WORLD"*?

- Jesus said, *"I am the Light of the world; the one who follows Me will not walk in the darkness, but will have the Light of life"* (John 8:12).

- The above verse says followers of Christ should no longer walk in darkness which is a reference to sin. In other words, since Jesus is Light, then believers should no longer live in sin because light and dark cannot coexist.

- Christians should reflect the Light in every area of their lives so that nonbelievers will see the love of Christ lived out in the believer's life.

(Q) WHAT IS *"THE DAY OF CHRIST"*?

- This will be a time of joy when God returns for His people. Christ's return will end the believers struggle against sin and death, and then God will distribute the believer's inheritance.

- The day of Christ is also known as the Rapture which will begin the seven years of the Tribulation (pre-trib view).

- Here is a simple timeline showing the Rapture and the Tribulation leading to the second coming of Jesus.

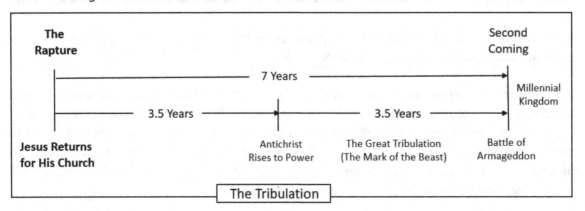

Let's RE-Read Tonight's Verses

Philippians 2:1-16 (NASB). [1] Therefore if there is any encouragement in Christ, if any consolation of love, if any fellowship of the Spirit, if any affection and compassion,

~~~~~~

[2] make my joy complete by being of the same mind, maintaining the same love, united in spirit, intent on one purpose.

~~~~~~

[3] Do nothing from selfishness or empty conceit, but with humility consider one another as more important than yourselves; [4] do not merely look out for your own personal interests, but also for the interests of others.

~~~~~~

[5] Have this attitude in yourselves which was also in Christ Jesus, [6] who, as He already existed in the form of God,

~~~~~~

did not consider equality with God something to be grasped, [7] but emptied Himself by taking the form of a bond-servant and being born in the likeness of men.

~~~~~~

[8] And being found in appearance as a man, He humbled Himself by becoming obedient to the point of death: death on a cross.

~~~~~~

[9] For this reason also God highly exalted Him, and bestowed on Him the name which is above every name,

~~~~~~

[10] so that at the name of Jesus every knee will bow, of those who are in heaven and on earth and under the earth, [11] and that every tongue will confess that Jesus Christ is Lord, to the glory of God the Father.

~~~~~~

[12] So then, my beloved, just as you have always obeyed, not as in my presence only, but now much more in my absence, work out your own salvation with fear and trembling;

~~~~~~

[13] for it is God who is at work in you, both to desire and to work for His good pleasure.

~~~~~~

[14] Do all things without complaining or arguments; [15] so that you will prove yourselves to be blameless and innocent,

~~~~~~

children of God above reproach in the midst of a crooked and perverse generation, among whom you appear as lights in the world,

~~~~~~

[16] holding firmly the word of life, so that on the day of Christ I can take pride because I did not run in vain nor labor in vain.

(Q) ANY FINAL COMMENTS? _____

This is the end of this week's study.

Notes

Philippians:
Rejoice in the Lord

WEEK 4 - PHILIPPIANS 2:17-30

Let's Review Last Week's Study

Last week, Paul continued to address the conflict threatening to divide the church by encouraging the Philippians to have the same attitude as Jesus did (Philippians 2:6). Then he reminded them that everyone will give an account of their lives at the **Bema Seat of Christ**. This was to encourage the Philippians to obey the Lord by "*working out their own salvation with fear and trembling.*"

The key verses from last week were to "*do all things without complaining or arguments; so that you will prove yourselves to be blameless and innocent, children of God above reproach in the midst of a crooked and perverse generation, among whom you appear as lights in the world*" (Philippians 2:14-15). Doesn't this sound a lot like the world we live in today?

(Q) WHAT DID PAUL MEAN WHEN HE SAID "*WORK OUT YOUR SALVATION*"? _____

(Q) ANY COMMENTS ON LAST WEEK'S STUDY? _____

Stop and discuss the above comments and questions — Answer to questions are on the next page.

Let's Review Tonight's Study

Paul starts off tonight by comparing his imprisonment and potential execution to an ancient Jewish tradition were the high priest poured a drink offering over an animal while it was being prepared as a sacrifice to God. So when Paul said he was being poured out as a drink offering, he was saying that he believed his execution was near.

Then he let the Philippians know that he would be sending his close friend Timothy to Philippi so he could see how they were doing in their Christian walk. Paul was expecting Timothy's report would bring him encouragement because of how well the Philippians were doing.

As Paul made plans to send Timothy, he reminded the Philippians to **involve God in their own plans**; otherwise, if God doesn't bless their plans, they are wasting their time. Another plan that Paul had was to send Epaphroditus back home to Philippi. Epaphroditus was in Rome because he delivered supplies and money to Paul, and then he stayed to take care of him. While in Rome, Epaphroditus got very sick and almost died. After he recovered, Paul decided to send him back home to be with his family so they wouldn't worry about him.

Timothy and Epaphroditus were leaders in their respective churches and as leaders they were at risk of all sorts of spiritual attacks. Therefore, Paul encouraged the Philippians to "*receive [them] in the Lord with all joy, and hold people like [them] in high regard*" (Philippians 2:29). Later tonight, we will discuss the requirements and responsibilities for church leadership.

Reflective Question*: Do you involve God in your plans before you make them?*

(Q) WHAT CAN YOU DO WHEN UNDER SPIRITUAL ATTACK? _____

(Q) ANY COMMENTS? _____

Stop and discuss the above comments and questions — Answer to questions are on the next page.

Answers to Questions from the Previous Page

(Q) WHAT DID PAUL MEAN WHEN HE SAID *"WORK OUT YOUR SALVATION"*?

- Paul was encouraging the Philippians to put real effort into their Christian walk.

- He did not mean for them to work **for** their salvation, but rather to work **out** their salvation.

- When a believer works out their salvation, the fruit of the Spirit will be evident in every area of their life and people will know them by their love for one another (John 13:35).

(Q) WHAT CAN YOU DO WHEN UNDER SPIRITUAL ATTACK?

- Turn to the Lord in prayer. Ask others to pray with you and for you.

- Prepare for battle and put on the full armor of God (Ephesians 6:10-18). A spiritual battle must be fought with spiritual weapons and not our own human effort (2 Corinthians 10:3-4).

- Be careful not to label every problem or conflict a spiritual attack. Sometimes they are the result of your own sinful behavior or someone else's sinful behavior.

Let's Begin Tonight's Study

> **Philippians 2:17-18 (NASB).** [17] But even if **I am being poured out as a drink offering** upon the sacrifice and service of your faith, I **rejoice** and share my joy with you all. [18] You too, I urge you, **rejoice** in the same way and share your joy with me.

Commentary. Paul's comment about "*being poured out as a drink offering*" would have reminded the Jews of their ancient practice of pouring wine or perfume over an animal sacrificed to God (Numbers 28:7). Remember, Paul was imprisoned and awaiting trial and there was the real possibility that he would be executed for crimes he did not commit. Therefore, when Paul said, "*I am being poured out as a drink offering,*" he was referring to the likelihood of being executed and put to death. Paul wanted the believers to share in his joy of possibility dying and going to heaven to be with the Lord. The Message Bible says "*Join me in my rejoicing [and] whatever you do, don't feel sorry for me*" (Philippians 2:18 MSG).

What about Christians today? Is it possible for them to live their life as a **living sacrifice** to the Lord? Yes it is. In Paul's letter to the Romans, he said, "*offer your bodies as a living sacrifice, holy and pleasing to God*" (Romans 12:1 NIV).

(Q) HOW CAN A BELIEVER'S LIFE BE A "LIVING SACRIFICE"? _____

(Q) ANY COMMENTS ON THESES VERSES? _____

Stop and discuss the above verses and questions — Answer to questions are on the next page.

> **Philippians 2:19 (NASB).** [19] I hope in the Lord Jesus, **to send Timothy to you** shortly, so that I also may be encouraged when I learn of your condition.

Commentary. We met Timothy during Paul's first missionary journey through Galatia when Timothy was just a young boy. On Paul's second missionary journey he asked Timothy to join him and Silas as they traveled to Philippi. This meant that Timothy was in Philippi during the church's infancy. Timothy had a good relationship with the Philippians and over the years he visited them several times (Acts 19:21-22; 20:3-6). In this verse, Paul was letting the Philippians know that he was sending Timothy to them.

Paul mentored him and they were partners in the mission field. Timothy pastored the church at Ephesus (1 Timothy 1:3) and co-authored six epistles with Paul (2 Corinthians, Philippians, Colossians, 1 and 2 Thessalonians, and Philemon).

Reflective Question: Do you have a mentor and do you mentor new believers?

(Q) WHAT DID PAUL MEAN IN VERSE 19b WHEN HE SAID "*SO THAT 'I' MAY BE ENCOURAGED*"?
_____

(Q) ANY COMMENTS ON THESES VERSES? _____

Stop and discuss the above verses and questions — Answer to questions are on the next page.

Answers to Questions from the Previous Page

(Q) HOW CAN A BELIEVER'S LIFE BE A "LIVING SACRIFICE"?

The verse said, "*Offer your bodies as a living sacrifice, holy and pleasing to God*" (Romans 12:1 NIV).

- Let's start by defining the word sacrifice. According to the dictionary, sacrifice means the act of offering something valuable to a deity. The sacrifice must cost the giver something of importance. In this case, the thing of importance is the believer's life.

- In the next verse, Paul described what this involves when he said, "*do not be conformed to this world, but be transformed by the renewing of your mind, so that you may prove what the will of God is, that which is good and acceptable and perfect*" (Romans 12:2).

- The transformation of the believer's mind from worldliness to Godliness can only be done through the power of the Holy Spirit and reading Gods Word.

(Q) WHAT DID PAUL MEAN IN VERSE 19b WHEN HE SAID "*SO THAT 'I' MAY BE ENCOURAGED*"?

- Paul wanted to send Timothy to Philippi so he could get a report on how well the Philippians were doing in their faith.

- Paul expected the report to be positive and thereby bring him joy and encouragement in knowing how well they were doing without him.

- Contrast this to Paul's letter to the Corinthians where he expected to hear bad news because the Corinthians were struggling with sin and false teachers (2 Corinthians 13:2-3).

> **Philippians 2:20 (NASB).** [20] For I have no one else of **kindred spirit** who will genuinely be concerned for your welfare.

Commentary. Paul led Timothy to the Lord during one of his missionary journeys and it was clear that he trusted Timothy and loved him like his own son (1 Timothy 1:2). In these verses, Paul described his friendship with Timothy as "*kindred spirits.*" The dictionary defines kindred spirits as friends who have the same opinions, feelings, interests, and worldview. Paul was assuring the Philippians that he was sending Timothy because he "*genuinely*" cared about their wellbeing. The dictionary defines genuine as someone who is sincere, honest, truthful, and is free from hypocrisy. Genuine friendships are hard to find, wouldn't you agree?

Reflective Question: Would your friends say that you are a "genuine friend" or an "acquaintance"?

(Q) DO YOU HAVE A FRIEND THAT YOU WOULD CALL A "*KINDRED SPIRIT*"? DESCRIBE THIS RELATIONSHIP. _____

(Q) ANY COMMENTS ON THESES VERSES? _____

Stop and discuss the above verses and questions — Answer to questions are on the next page.

> **Philippians 2:21-22 (NASB).** [21] **For they all seek after their own interests**, not those of Christ Jesus. [22] But you know of [Timothy's] proven character, that he served with me in the furtherance of the gospel like a child serving his father.

Commentary. Paul just finished telling the Philippians that by sending Timothy, he was sending someone he knew could serve as a surrogate pastor in his place. Timothy was not a new believer and his faith had stood the test of time. In these verses, Paul was expressing his concern that there were some people around him who were serving their own interests and not those of the Lord.

How does this apply today?
When someone wants to be a leader in the church, they should be vetted against the requirements listed in the Bible. For example, an **overseer**, also called a pastor, bishop or elder, must meet the specific qualifications outlined in 1 Timothy 3:2-7 and Titus 1:6-9. They have the responsibility of overseeing the flock that has been entrusted to them, and should have a heart of servanthood. On the other hand, someone wishing to **lead a ministry** should be vetted against the requirements listed in 1 Timothy 3:8-13. Serving in the church is a serious responsibility and should not be taken lightly or rushed into.

(Q) WHY SHOULD THE CHURCH BE SLOW IN APPOINTING SOMEONE TO A POSITION OF LEADERSHIP? _____

(Q) ANY COMMENTS ON THESES VERSES? _____

Stop and discuss the above verses and questions — Answer to questions are on the next page.

Answers to Questions from the Previous Page

(Q) DO YOU HAVE A FRIEND THAT YOU WOULD CALL A *"KINDRED SPIRIT"*? DESCRIBE THIS RELATIONSHIP.

- Testimony time.

- Ask a couple of people to share the attributes that make these relationships different than other relationships.

- Limit sharing to 2-3 minutes.

(Q) WHY SHOULD THE CHURCH BE SLOW IN APPOINTING SOMEONE TO A POSITION OF LEADERSHIP?

- Those who are called to lead God's people are called into servant leadership in the same way Jesus modeled when He washed the disciple's feet (John 13:5-11).

- A person desiring a leadership position in the church must not be a new convert and must meet the requirements outlined in 1 Timothy for overseers, pastors, bishops, elders and deacons.

- According to the Bible, church leadership is not about controlling people, but is about serving the congregation (Mark 10:43).

- Leadership appointees must pass the test of time, meaning they have a track record of serving and are not new converts.

> **Philippians 2:23-24 (NASB).** [23] Therefore I hope to send him immediately, as soon as I see how things go with me; [24] and **I trust in the Lord** that I myself will also be coming shortly.

Commentary. As Paul awaited his fate, he wrote this letter to let the Philippians know he was sending Timothy to them so they could report the amazing things God was doing in and through them. Paul also wanted them to know that he was planning on visiting Philippi, *if it was the Lords will.*

How does this apply today? When a believer makes plans and operates out of their own willpower, their plans are sure to fail if God is not involved. The Apostle James said *"You do not know what your life will be like tomorrow. For you are just a vapor that appears for a little while, and then vanishes away. Instead, you ought to say, 'If the Lord wills, we will live and also do this or that'"* (James 4:14-15).

In other words, James was imploring Christians to live their lives with faith that God is in control. After all, nothing can happen unless God blesses it, or as the old joke goes; "if you want to make God laugh, tell Him your plans."

Reflective Question: Do you boast in your plans and accomplishments, instead of giving God the glory?

(Q) WHAT WAS PAUL WAITING FOR IN VERSE 23? _____

(Q) ANY COMMENTS ON THESES VERSES? _____

Stop and discuss the above verses and questions — Answer to questions are on the next page.

> **Philippians 2:25-26 (NASB).** [25] But I thought it necessary **to send to you Epaphroditus**, my brother and fellow worker and fellow soldier, who is also your messenger and minister to my need, [26] because he was longing for you all and was **upset because you had heard that he was sick**.

Commentary. Epaphroditus was a Greek who was a messenger sent by the Philippians to bring money and supplies to Paul, and to minister to Paul's needs while he was in prison. Epaphroditus got sick while he was taking care of Paul. After he recovered from his sickness, he became upset when he heard that his family and friends were worried about him. So Paul decided to send Epaphroditus back home to Philippi and at the same time deliver this letter to the Philippians.

Paul called Epaphroditus his brother in Christ even though he was a Greek and Paul was Jewish. In God's eyes, *"There is neither Jew nor Greek, there is neither slave nor free, there is neither male nor female; for you are all one in Christ Jesus"* (Galatians 3:28).

(Q) WHAT DOES IT MEAN *"THERE ARE NEITHER JEW NOR GENTILE"*? _____
_____

(Q) ANY COMMENTS ON THESES VERSES? _____

Stop and discuss the above verses and questions — Answer to questions are on the next page.

Answers to Questions from the Previous Page

(Q) WHAT WAS PAUL WAITING FOR IN VERSE 23?

> **Philippians 2:23 (NIV).** 23 Therefore I hope to send him immediately, **as soon as I see how things go with me**.

- Paul was on house arrest awaiting trial for crimes he supposedly committed in Jerusalem. We know from the book of Acts that he was innocent of these charges.

- Therefore, this verse means that Paul was waiting for the outcome of his trial before sending Timothy to Philippi.

- We know from the Pastoral Epistles that Paul was eventually released from prison and while he was free, he went to Macedonia and Crete before returning to Rome. There are three Pastoral Epistles: 1 Timothy, 2 Timothy, and Titus.

(Q) WHAT DOES IT MEAN *"THERE ARE NEITHER JEW NOR GENTILE"*?

> **Galatians 3:28 (NIV).** 28 There is **neither Jew nor Gentile**, neither slave nor free, nor is there male and female, for you are all one in Christ Jesus.

- God sees the world differently than humans do. He does **not** see age, nor race, nor sex, nor does He judge people based on looks or money.

- What God sees are believers and nonbelievers. All believers are equal heirs according to the covenant God made with Abraham, and all believers are brothers and sisters in Christ.

- This would have bothered some Jewish Christians because for years the Jews have been taught that they are God's chosen people, and everyone else was a pagan.

Philippians 2:27 (NASB). ²⁷ For indeed he was sick to the point of death, but God had mercy on him, and not only on him but also on me, so that I would not have **sorrow upon sorrow**.

Commentary. Epaphroditus was so sick that he almost died. We know that Timothy and doctor Luke were with Paul in Rome and probably provided medical assistance to him, but ultimately, it was God who had mercy and healed him.

Does God still heal people today? Yes, of course He does, but not everyone who needs healing is healed. Why not, why does God heal some people but not others? This is one of those mysteries that cannot be fully understood. Paul tried to answer this question by quoting the Old Testament where God said to Moses, "'*I will show mercy and compassion to anyone I choose.' So it is God who decides to show mercy. We can neither choose it nor work for it*" (Romans 9:15-16 NLT). In other words, God works all things together based on His sovereignty (Romans 8:28).

(Q) WHAT DID PAUL MEAN WHEN HE SAID *"SO THAT I WOULD NOT HAVE SORROW UPON SORROW"*?

_____

(Q) ANY COMMENTS ON THESES VERSES? _____

Stop and discuss the above verses and questions — Answer to questions are on the next page.

Philippians 2:28-30 (NASB). ²⁸ Therefore I have sent him all the more eagerly, so that when you see him again you may rejoice and I may be less concerned about you. ²⁹ Receive him then in the Lord with all joy, **and hold people like him in high regard**, ³⁰ because he came close to death for the work of Christ, risking his life to compensate for your absence in your service to me.

Commentary. The Philippians were upset when they heard Epaphroditus was sick and almost died. We do not know the nature of Epaphroditus's illness other than it was serious. In these verses, Paul was letting the Philippians know that he was sending Epaphroditus home and encouraged them to rejoice and give him a hero's welcome for risking his life in service to the Lord.

How does this apply today? It is easy to treat **first responders** as hero's for risking their lives in service to others, but what about the missionary who risks their life bringing Bibles and supplies into dangerous places? They are heroes as well, but may not be rewarded in this life, and sometimes they are persecuted for their efforts. Warren Wiersbe says, "*the problem in our churches today is that we have too many spectators and not enough participants.*"

Reflective Question: Are you a spectator or a participant in your church?

(Q) WHAT KINDS OF PEOPLE DOES THE WORLD LOOK UP TO AS IT'S HEROES? _____

_____

(Q) ANY COMMENTS ON THESES VERSES? _____

Stop and discuss the above verses and questions — Answer to questions are on the next page.

Answers to Questions from the Previous Page

(Q) WHAT DID PAUL MEAN WHEN HE SAID *"SO THAT I WOULD NOT HAVE SORROW UPON SORROW"*?

- Paul's first sorrow referred to his circumstances of being wrongly imprisoned and beaten multiple times to the point of near death for preaching the Word of God.

- His second sorrow referred to the possibility of Epaphroditus dying. If he had died, Paul would have been grieving the loss of his friend as well as grieving his own circumstances.

- In other words, he would have had *"sorrow upon sorrow."*

(Q) WHAT KINDS OF PEOPLE DOES THE WORLD LOOK UP TO AS IT'S HEROES?

- The dictionary defines "hero" as a person who is admired or idolized for courage, outstanding achievements, or noble qualities.

- My definition of "hero" is someone who gives of themselves for the benefit of another person.

- The world admires people based on looks, money, power, athletics, success and intelligence.

- Just look at television for some examples of how twisted the world has become. There are TV shows where the winners are rewarded for lying and deceiving better than the other contestants. And the "news" reports that men and women are courageous for changing their sex, and then they create TV shows where men dress up as women to compete as drag queens.

- Maybe the worst example of misplaced adoration is the worship of self. In this modern age of selfies and social media, people post photoshopped pictures of themselves and exaggerated descriptions of their wonderful lives to impress people they don't even know. In other words, they are their own heroes.

- Jesus gave His life for the salvation of the world. He is the ultimate hero in my life. How about your hero?

Let's RE-Read Tonight's Verses

Philippians 2:17-30 (NASB). [17] But even if I am being poured out as a drink offering upon the sacrifice and service of your faith, I rejoice and share my joy with you all.

~~~~~~

[18] You too, I urge you, rejoice in the same way and share your joy with me.

~~~~~~

[19] But I hope, in the Lord Jesus, to send Timothy to you shortly, so that I also may be encouraged when I learn of your condition.

~~~~~~

[20] For I have no one else of kindred spirit who will genuinely be concerned for your welfare.

~~~~~~

[21] For they all seek after their own interests, not those of Christ Jesus.

~~~~~~

[22] But you know of his proven character, that he served with me in the furtherance of the gospel like a child serving his father.

~~~~~~

[23] Therefore I hope to send him immediately, as soon as I see how things go with me; [24] and I trust in the Lord that I myself will also be coming shortly.

~~~~~~

[25] But I thought it necessary to send to you Epaphroditus, my brother and fellow worker and fellow soldier, who is also your messenger and minister to my need,

~~~~~~

[26] because he was longing for you all and was distressed because you had heard that he was sick.

~~~~~~

[27] For indeed he was sick to the point of death, but God had mercy on him, and not only on him but also on me, so that I would not have sorrow upon sorrow.

~~~~~~

[28] Therefore I have sent him all the more eagerly, so that when you see him again you may rejoice and I may be less concerned about you.

~~~~~~

[29] Receive him then in the Lord with all joy, and hold people like him in high regard,

~~~~~~

[30] because he came close to death for the work of Christ, risking his life to compensate for your absence in your service to me.

(Q) ANY FINAL COMMENTS? _____

This is the end of this week's study.

Notes

68

Philippians: Rejoice in the Lord

WEEK 5 - PHILIPPIANS 3:1-11

Let's Review Last Week's Study

We finished last week with Paul responding to the Philippians concern for their friend Epaphroditus who they heard was sick and almost died. Paul wrote to let the Philippians know that Epaphroditus had recovered from his illness and would be coming home soon.

Then Paul let the Philippians know that he was going to send Timothy to visit them on his behalf so they could give him an update on their ministry. Paul was expecting Timothy's report to be positive, and therefore, it would bring him encouragement. He also wanted to let them know that he was planning on going to Philippi to visit them.

However, his plan to leave Rome was dependent on the outcome of his court case. He compared his imprisonment and potential execution to the ancient Jewish tradition of pouring a drink offering over an animal being prepared as a sacrifice to God. Even though there was a chance that Paul would be executed, he was confident that God would work out his situation so that he would be freed from prison.

Then he reminded the Philippian believers to involve God in all their plans, otherwise without God, their plans were doomed to fail. This advice still applies to us today. As the Apostle James said, "*You do not know what your life will be like tomorrow. For you are just a vapor that appears for a little while, and then vanishes away. Instead, you ought to say, 'If the Lord wills, we will live and also do this or that'*" (James 4:14-15).

(Q) WHY WAS EPAPHRODITUS IN ROME? _____

(Q) ANY COMMENTS ON LAST WEEK'S STUDY? _____

Stop and discuss the above comments and questions — Answer to questions are on the next page.

Let's Review Tonight's Study

We start out with a warning from Paul about some false teachers in the church at Philippi who were preaching a works-based doctrine. These false teachers were preaching that faith in Jesus was not enough for salvation and that the Jewish and Gentile Christians must be circumcised and follow the Jewish traditions. In other words, they were putting their faith in their own human efforts for salvation rather than in Jesus.

Paul addressed this by telling the Philippians, "*I myself could boast as having confidence in the flesh. If anyone else thinks he is confident in the flesh, I have more reason*" (Philippians 3:4). If anyone could earn their way into heaven based on their own human efforts and credentials, it was Paul. But then he said, "*I put no confidence in the flesh.*" He was using himself to make the point that salvation was faith in Jesus and nothing else.

(Q) WHAT DO YOU KNOW ABOUT "*PAUL'S JEWISH CREDENTIALS*"? _____

(Q) ANY COMMENTS? _____

Stop and discuss the above comments and questions — Answer to questions are on the next page.

Answers to Questions from the Previous Page

(Q) WHY WAS EPAPHRODITUS IN ROME?

- The churches in Philippi sent Epaphroditus to deliver money and supplies to Paul.

- After he delivered the supplies, Epaphroditus stayed in Rome to tend to Paul's needs.

- While he was helping Paul, he got sick and almost died.

- After he recovered, Paul sent him home to deliver this letter to the Philippians.

- Epaphroditus was a hero for giving of himself for the benefit of Paul.

(Q) WHAT DO YOU KNOW ABOUT *"PAUL'S JEWISH CREDENTIALS"*?

- Before Paul became a Christian, he was known as Saul of Tarsus and was persecuting and killing followers of **the Way** (Acts 8). In ancient Israel, the early Christians were called followers of the Way.

- Saul of Tarsus was from the tribe of Benjamin and trained under Rabbi Gamaliel (Acts 22:3).

- He was a Roman citizen and a Pharisee who was highly educated in the upper ranks of Judaism.

- He was a member of the Sanhedrin Council (Philippians 3:5-6).

- Here is how Paul described his Jewish credentials: *"I was circumcised the eighth day, of the nation of Israel, of the tribe of Benjamin, a Hebrew of Hebrews; as to the Law, a Pharisee; as to zeal, a persecutor of the church; as to the righteousness which is in the Law, found blameless"* (Philippians 3:5-6).

Let's Begin Tonight's Study

> **Philippians 3:1-3 (NASB).** [1] Finally, my brothers and sisters, rejoice in the Lord. To write the same things again is no trouble for me, and it is a safeguard for you. [2] Beware of the dogs, beware of the evil workers, **beware of the false circumcision**; [3] **for we are the true circumcision**, who worship in the Spirit of God and take pride in Christ Jesus.

Commentary. In these verses, Paul made it clear that he wanted the Philippians full attention because he was about to share something very important. We know this because he said, "*to write the same things again is no trouble for me.*" Before giving them this very important message, he reminded the believers again to "*rejoice in the Lord*" in spite of the trouble around them. The trouble was that some Jewish Christians were causing division in the church. How do we know the troublemakers were Jewish Christians and not the Gentile Christians? The answer is that Paul said to "*beware of the false circumcision.*" When the Bible mentions the circumcised, it is referring to the covenant that God made with Abraham and the nation of Israel, which meant he was referring to the Jew's who had converted to Christianity.

Therefore, when Paul said to "*beware of the false circumcision,*" he was warning the Philippians about some Jews in the church who were preaching a false doctrine. They were insisting the Gentiles get circumcised and follow the Jewish traditions if they wanted to be saved. In other words, the "*false circumcision*" were claiming the Gentiles must become Jews before they could become Christians.

This was the same problem that Paul faced with the Judaizers during his first missionary journey through Galatia. As a reminder, when Paul returned from Galatia, he brought this problem up to the elders in a meeting called the Council at Jerusalem. The result of this meeting was a letter that was sent to all the churches refuting the Judaizers teachings.

Paul called these false teachers "dogs," which is the same term the Jews used to call Gentiles before Jesus came. Who says Paul didn't have a sense of humor? He described the real Christians as "*the true circumcision.*" This is the same thing Paul said to the Romans when he described the true believers as those who have had a "*circumcision of the heart*" (Romans 2:28-29).

(Q) WHAT DOES "*CIRCUMCISION OF THE HEART*" MEAN? _____

(Q) ANY COMMENTS ON THESES VERSES? _____

Stop and discuss the above verses and questions — Answer to questions are on the next page.

Answers to Questions from the Previous Page

(Q) WHAT DOES "*CIRCUMCISION OF THE HEART*" MEAN?

- The NLT Bible described it as "*a change of heart produced by the Spirit, and a person with a changed heart seeks praise from God, not from people*" (Romans 2:29 NLT).

- Therefore, "*the true circumcision*" were the Jewish believers who have had a change of heart and understood that salvation was faith in Jesus and nothing else.

- However, if some Jews chose to follow their Jewish traditions, including circumcision, it was okay as long as they realized these traditions were not conditions for salvation, and the Gentiles were not required to follow them.

> **Philippians 3:4-7 (NASB).** I put no confidence in the flesh. ⁴ Although I myself could boast as having confidence even in the flesh. **If anyone else thinks he is confident in the flesh, I have more reason**: ⁵ circumcised the eighth day, of the nation of Israel, of the tribe of Benjamin, a Hebrew of Hebrews; as to the Law, a Pharisee. ⁶ As to zeal, a persecutor of the church; as to the righteousness which is in the Law, found blameless. ⁷ But whatever things were gain to me, these things **I have counted as loss** because of Christ.

Commentary. In these verses, Paul laid out his credentials as a Jew in the upper ranks of Judaism. Before continuing, let's discuss the Jewish culture. Jews who spoke Hebrew looked down on Jews who lived outside of Jerusalem and spoke Greek instead of their native Hebrew language. Since Paul was raised in Tarsus, a Greek city, he was a Roman citizen and spoke Greek. However, he was educated in Jerusalem by the Rabbi Gamaliel and therefore spoke Hebrew. He was also a Pharisee and a member of the Sanhedrin Council which consisted of 70 members and served as the supreme court for all Jewish issues.

Why was this important? Three reasons: (1) Paul's credentials would have made him elite in the eyes of the Jews, (2) knowing Greek would allow him to share the good news with the Gentiles, and (3) he would have had the respect of the Romans because he was a Roman citizen. Therefore, Paul was uniquely qualified to share the gospel with all types of people: Jews, Greeks and Romans.

(Q) WHAT POINT WAS PAUL MAKING IN VERSE 7? _____

(Q) ANY COMMENTS ON THESES VERSES? _____

Stop and discuss the above verses and questions — Answer to questions are on the next page.

Before moving to the next set of verses, let's reread verse 6 and continue our discussion on Paul's credentials as a Jew in the upper ranks of Judaism.

> **Philippians 3:6a (NASB).** ⁶ As to **zeal**, a persecutor of the church.

Commentary. In this short verse, Paul was emphasizing his **zeal** for the Jewish faith when he was Saul of Tarsus. Zealous means having a fervent passion for a cause or ideal. Saul, now the Apostle Paul, was definitely a zealous Jew. In his letter to the Galatians, he described himself as, *"advancing in Judaism beyond many of my contemporaries among my countrymen, being more extremely zealous for my ancestral traditions"* (Galatians 1:14).

Reflective Question: Do you have a zeal for sharing the gospel with the lost?

(Q) WHAT DID PAUL MEAN WHEN HE SAID HE WAS A *"PERSECUTOR OF THE CHURCH"*? _____
_____

(Q) ANY COMMENTS ON THESES VERSES? _____

Stop and discuss the above verses and questions — Answer to questions are on the next page.

Answers to Questions from the Previous Page

(Q) WHAT POINT WAS PAUL MAKING IN VERSE 7?

> **Philippians 3:7 (NASB).** [7] *But whatever things were gain to me, these things **I have counted as loss** because of Christ*

- Paul laid out his very impressive Jewish credentials to show that if anyone could earn their way into heaven based on human effort, it was him. But then he said none of these matters when it comes to Christ. His accomplishments are insignificant.

- Another translation said it this way: *"I once thought these things were valuable, but now I consider them worthless because of what Christ has done. Yes, everything else is worthless when compared with the infinite value of knowing Christ Jesus my Lord. For His sake I have discarded everything else, counting it all as garbage, so that I could gain Christ and become one with Him"* (Philippians 3:7-8 NLT).

(Q) WHAT DID PAUL MEAN WHEN HE SAID HE WAS A *"PERSECUTOR OF THE CHURCH"*?

- Before Jesus met Saul on the road to Damascus, he was a zealous Jew and believed the Christians were a threat to the Jewish faith. As he said in Galatians, *"I'm sure that you've heard the story of my earlier life when I lived in the Jewish way. In those days I went all out in persecuting God's church. I was systematically destroying it"* (Galatians 1:13 MSG).

- Paul never forgot how he tried to destroy the church. In his letter to the Corinthians he said, *"For I am the least of the apostles, and not fit to be called an apostle, because I persecuted the church of God"* (1 Corinthians 15:9 NLT).

- Paul was not boasting about persecuting the church, but was making the point that he was passionate about his faith.

Let's reread the second part of verse 6 so we can finish our discussion on Paul's credentials.

> **Philippians 3:6b (NASB).** As to the **righteousness** which is in the Law, found blameless.

Commentary. In the Sermon on the Mount, Jesus said, *"For I say to you that unless your righteousness far surpasses that of the scribes and Pharisees, you will not enter the kingdom of heaven"* (Matthew 5:20). Paul was making a case that when he was Saul of Tarsus, his righteousness exceeded the scribes and Pharisees. Yes, Paul was a member of the strictest religious sect in ancient Israel, the Pharisees, and yes it was true that he had done everything humanly possible to obey the Law. He was a Hebrew of Hebrews, and according to the righteousness in the Law, he was blameless. However, we know that the righteousness of man is not enough to enter God's perfect kingdom.

How does this apply today? Some people like to imitate the Pharisees by boasting and displaying their righteous acts in public or on social media to show how holy they are. Jesus warned believers, *"Take care not to practice your righteousness in the sight of people, to be noticed by them; otherwise you have no reward with your Father who is in heaven"* (Matthew 6:1).

(Q) WHAT IS *"THE LAW"*? _____

(Q) ANY COMMENTS ON THESES VERSES? _____

Stop and discuss the above verses and questions — Answer to questions are on the next page.

Now, let's find out *why* Paul shared his credentials with the Jewish Christians.

> **Philippians 3:8 (NASB).** [8] More than that, **I count all things to be loss** in view of the surpassing value of knowing Christ Jesus my Lord, for whom I have suffered the loss of all things, and count them **mere rubbish**.

Commentary. Of all the early Christians, Paul may have lost the most. Thirty years earlier, he was a Jew in the upper ranks of Judaism and was well respected and feared, and then Jesus met him on the road to Damascus and called him to be the apostle to the Gentiles. When Paul received Christ, he was ostracized by his friends and peers, and yet, he counted his old life as rubbish. Fast forward thirty years and he was still counting his old life as loss, and even called it worthless compared to the glory of God.

How many believers can say the same thing? Too many modern-day Christians have had a conversion experience and are on fire for the Lord, and then over time, they drift back into their old life style while compromising their faith. This is the reason nonbelievers call Christian's hypocrites. They see them leave their old life, only to return to their sinful ways praising Jesus along the way. What kind of witness is that?

(Q) WHAT DOES IT MEAN FOR CHRISTIANS TO *"COUNT ALL THINGS AS LOST"*? _____
_____

(Q) ANY COMMENTS ON THESES VERSES? _____

Stop and discuss the above verses and questions — Answer to questions are on the next page.

Answers to Questions from the Previous Page

(Q) WHAT IS "*THE LAW*"?

The Law is also called the **Law of Moses** and consists of over 600 commandments and regulations that are contained in the first five books of the Bible. The Law can be divided into three groups:

- **The Moral Laws.** These include the Ten Commandments that God gave to Moses on Mount Sinai.

- **The Civil (Judicial) Laws.** These are the laws that govern the Jewish society.

- **The Ceremonial Laws.** These are the Jewish ceremonies for sacrifices, rituals, cleanliness, and festivals.

(Q) WHAT DOES IT MEAN FOR CHRISTIANS TO "*COUNT ALL THINGS AS LOST*"?

- Let's start with the Apostle Paul. He gave up his high status in the Jewish society, including his reputation, to follow Jesus. He also gave up his home, financial security and friends. What he gained was the righteousness of God through faith in Jesus. In other words, Paul considered everything he lost as worthless compared to what he gained in Christ.

- In the Gospel of Matthew, Jesus told the rich young ruler "*If you want to be complete, go and sell your possessions and give to the poor, and you will have treasure in heaven; and come, follow Me*" (Matthew 19:21). Jesus was telling the rich young ruler to give up everything that he valued greater than Christ.

- In the Old Testament, God told Abraham to sacrifice his son Isaac. Abraham loved Isaac more than anything, but he obeyed God and took his son to the land of Moriah to sacrifice him.

- Why would God require such a high cost? The reason is because this is the cost Jesus paid for the forgiveness of sin and the salvation of His people.

- The Bible says Christians must be willing to lose everything: their wealth, family, friends, status in society, in exchange for obedience and faith in Christ.

- The Message Bible said it this way: "*The very credentials these people are waving around as something special, I'm tearing up and throwing out with the trash, along with everything else I used to take credit for. And why? Because of Christ. Yes, all the things I once thought were so important are gone from my life. Compared to the high privilege of knowing Christ Jesus as my Master, firsthand, everything I once thought I had going for me is insignificant, [like] dog dung. I've dumped it all in the trash so that I could embrace Christ and be embraced by Him*" (Philippians 3:7-8 MSG).

> **Philippians 3:9 (NASB).** So that I may gain Christ, ⁹ and may be found in Him, **not having a righteousness of my own derived from the Law,** but that which is through faith in Christ, the righteousness which comes from God on the basis of faith.

Commentary. Paul continued to emphasize how futile it was for a person to try and earn their righteousness through human effort. If a person cannot earn their salvation by obeying the Law, then what was the purpose of the Law to begin with? The Law defined God's holy standard and made people aware of their sin, and thus their need for a savior. In that respect, the Law served as a guardian to show people God's moral boundaries of right and wrong behavior. In Paul's letter to the Galatians, he wrote, *"the Law has become our guardian **to lead us to Christ**, so that we may be justified by faith. But now that faith has come, we are no longer under a guardian"* (Galatians 3:24-25).

Without the Law, people wouldn't know what sin is. Therefore, the Law revealed to a person the depth of their sins and showed them their need for a savior. The Law did what God intended it to do, and that was to bring the sinner to Christ. In other words, a right relationship with God does not come from obeying the Law. It comes from repenting and putting your faith in Jesus for the forgiveness of sins.

Once a person is saved, they can do whatever they want to because of God's grace, right? *No that's not right!* Let's not forget what happens after salvation, which is sanctification.

(Q) WHAT IS THE DIFFERENCE BETWEEN *"SALVATION"* AND *"SANCTIFICATION"*? _____

_____

(Q) ANY COMMENTS ON THESES VERSES? _____

Stop and discuss the above verses and questions — Answer to questions are on the next page.

> **Philippians 3:10-11 (NASB).** ¹⁰ That I may know Him and **the power of His resurrection and the fellowship of His sufferings,** being conformed to His death; ¹¹ if somehow I may attain to the resurrection from the dead.

Commentary. In these verses, Paul may have ruffled a few feathers or at the very least, confused some people. How can a believer find power in suffering with Christ? It is easy to see how a person would experience power from the resurrection because they would be experiencing power over death. But power from suffering? Let's think about this. A person cannot experience the power of the resurrection unless they were first dead, right? Therefore, for a believer to experience the power of the resurrection, they must first experience death, or as the Bible says, they must die to self.

(Q) WHAT WAS PAUL'S REASON FOR WANTING TO *"SUFFER WITH CHRIST"*? _____

_____

(Q) ANY COMMENTS ON THESES VERSES? _____

Stop and discuss the above verses and questions — Answer to questions are on the next page.

Answers to Questions from the Previous Page

(Q) WHAT IS THE DIFFERENCE BETWEEN *"SALVATION"* AND *"SANCTIFICATION"*?

Salvation

- This is a one-time event that occurs the moment a person repents and puts their faith in Jesus.

- At the point of salvation, the person's sins are forgiven and they are **justified** before God.

- Baptism is an outward sign of what has already happened in the believer's heart and is not required for salvation. However, believers are encouraged to make a public declaration of their faith through baptism. Baptism is a picture of the believer's identification with Christ's death, burial, and resurrection.

Sanctification

- This is a life-long process that begins the moment a person accepts Jesus as their Lord and Savior.

- Another way to describe sanctification is it is the daily process of growing spiritually into maturity as God chips away at the sin in the believer's life.

(Q) WHAT WAS PAUL'S REASON FOR WANTING TO *"SUFFER WITH CHRIST"*?

- In verse 10, Paul said his desire was to **know Christ** and he was willing to experience the same suffering as Jesus did so **he could know Him more**.

- Even the apostles understood that it was an honor to suffer for Christ. In the book of Acts, Peter and the apostles were beaten and thrown in jail for preaching the Gospel. After they were flogged, the Sanhedrin Council ordered them not to speak in the name of Jesus and then they released them. *"So [the apostles] went on their way from the presence of the Council, **rejoicing that they had been considered worthy to suffer shame for His name**"* (Acts 5:40-42).

- The Christians greatest suffering comes from within as they battle their own selfish desires with surrendering to Christ. In whatever form suffering comes, the believer should embrace it as a badge of honor and a privilege like the apostles did.

- Jesus said, *"If anyone wants to come after Me, he must deny himself, take up his cross daily, and follow Me. For whoever wants to save his life will lose it, but whoever loses his life for My sake, this is the one who will save it"* (Luke 23-24). In ancient Israel, the cross symbolized death. Therefore, Jesus was saying that, in order to follow Him, you must be willing to die to self.

Let's RE-Read Tonight's Verses

Philippians 3:1-11 (NASB). [1] Finally, my brothers and sisters, rejoice in the Lord.

~~~~~~

To write the same things again is no trouble for me, and it is a safeguard for you.

~~~~~~

[2] Beware of the dogs, beware of the evil workers, beware of the false circumcision;

~~~~~~

[3] for we are the true circumcision, who worship in the Spirit of God and take pride in Christ Jesus,

~~~~~~

and put no confidence in the flesh, [4] although I myself could boast as having confidence even in the flesh.

~~~~~~

If anyone else thinks he is confident in the flesh, I have more reason:

~~~~~~

[5] circumcised the eighth day, of the nation of Israel, of the tribe of Benjamin, a Hebrew of Hebrews;

~~~~~~

as to the Law, a Pharisee; [6] as to zeal, a persecutor of the church;

~~~~~~

as to the righteousness which is in the Law, found blameless.

~~~~~~

[7] But whatever things were gain to me, these things I have counted as loss because of Christ.

~~~~~~

[8] More than that, I count all things to be loss in view of the surpassing value of knowing Christ Jesus my Lord,

~~~~~~

for whom I have suffered the loss of all things, and count them mere rubbish, so that I may gain Christ,

~~~~~~

[9] and may be found in Him, not having a righteousness of my own derived from the Law,

~~~~~~

but that which is through faith in Christ, the righteousness which comes from God on the basis of faith,

~~~~~~

[10] that I may know Him and the power of His resurrection and the fellowship of His sufferings,

~~~~~~

being conformed to His death; [11] if somehow I may attain to the resurrection from the dead.

(Q) ANY FINAL COMMENTS? _____

This is the end of this week's study.

Notes

Philippians:
Rejoice in the Lord

WEEK 6 - PHILIPPIANS 3:12-21

Let's Review Last Week's Study

Paul warned the churches in Philippi about some false teachers who were insisting the Gentiles get circumcised and follow the Jewish laws and traditions. These false teachers were preaching a **works-based salvation** and that faith in Jesus was not enough. In other words, they were putting their faith in their own human efforts for salvation rather than in Jesus.

Then Paul rattled off his own Jewish credentials in an attempt to show the Philippians that if anyone had the credentials to earn their salvation through human effort, it was him. But then he said, "*I put no confidence in the flesh.*" He was using himself to make the point that salvation could not be earned and that the only way was through faith in Jesus and nothing else.

Paul wrapped up his thoughts on this by saying "*The very credentials these people are waving around as something special, I'm tearing up and throwing out with the trash, along with everything else I used to take credit for. And why? Because of Christ. Yes, all the things I once thought were so important are gone from my life. Compared to the high privilege of knowing Christ Jesus as my Master, firsthand, everything I once thought I had going for me is insignificant, [like] dog dung. I've dumped it all in the trash so that I could embrace Christ and be embraced by Him*" (Philippians 3:7-8 MSG).

(Q) WHAT RELIGIOUS ORGANIZATIONS WRONGLY PREACH A "*WORKS-BASED SALVATION*"?

_____

(Q) ANY COMMENTS? _____

> **Stop and discuss the above comments and questions — Answer to questions are on the next page.**

Let's Review Tonight's Study

Paul finished this chapter by urging the **mature believers** to help resolve a problem that was threatening to divide the church. The problem started with a disagreement between two women and was causing the Philippians to take sides. Paul reminded the believers of their calling and to "*press on toward the goal for the prize of the upward call of God in Christ Jesus*" (Philippians 3:14).

Then Paul urged the Philippians to follow his example and to lean on the mature believers in the church. The NLT Bible said it this way, "*pattern your lives after mine, and learn from those who follow our example*" (Philippians 3:17 NLT). This is a model that can still be followed today. Pastors and church elders cannot do everything and mature believers can help by mentoring and discipling new believers.

Paul finished this chapter with a warning about people who were abusing their freedom in Christ by indulging in their flesh. He described them as enemies of God who were putting more value on worldly things then on their relationship with God.

Reflective Question: *Do you value your stuff more than your relationship with God? If we did an audit on your bank account and calendar, where would it show you spending your time and resources?*

(Q) ANY COMMENTS? _____

> **Stop and discuss the above comments.**

Answers to Questions from the Previous Page

(Q) WHAT RELIGIOUS ORGANIZATIONS WRONGLY PREACH A "*WORKS-BASED SALVATION*"?

- The most obvious religion that teaches a works-based salvation is Catholicism. According to their doctrine, a Catholic can perform works-based acts for the forgiveness of sins. Here are a couple of examples:

    o **Penance** is assigned by a priest for the forgiveness of sins. That is to say, a priest assigns a certain number of "Our Fathers" and "Hail Mary's" for the sinner to recite so they can "earn" forgiveness.

    o **Purgatory** is a temporary place where a Catholic goes when they die because they don't have enough "works" to make it into heaven. Therefore, they must wait in Purgatory until their family and friends pay their temporal penalty by praying for them. Purgatory is not in the Bible.

    o **Salvation** is based on good works rather than God's grace. This negates the sacrifice that Jesus made on the cross because if a person could earn their salvation through their own efforts, then there was no need for Jesus to go to the cross.

- All of these are in conflict with the Bible which says, "*People are counted as righteous, **not** because of their work, but because of their faith in God who forgives sinners*" (Romans 4:5 NLT). Therefore, Penance and Purgatory are works-based salvation which are in conflict with the Word of God.

Let's Begin Tonight's Study

> **Philippians 3:12 (NASB).** [12] Not that I have already grasped it all or have already become perfect, but **I press on** if I may also take hold of that for which I was even taken hold of by Christ Jesus.

Commentary. In these verses, Paul was talking about striving for perfection. When the Bible mentions perfection, it usually refers to **spiritual maturity** and not necessarily God's perfect standard.

We ended last week with Paul telling the Philippians that his righteousness came from Jesus Christ and not from his own efforts. Paul began this section by continuing to emphasize that he has **not** arrived, and that he was still pressing on to achieve the purpose that Jesus had for his life. No human can attain God's perfect standard, but they can strive for maturity in their faith. One-way believers can do this is to have an attitude of gratitude for the things of God, and to put God first in all things. As Pastor Chuck Smith said, *"When we consider who God is and what He has done for us, how can we do less than offer Him our best?"*

Reflective Question: Are you giving God your best, or are you giving Him your leftovers?

(Q) WHAT DOES IT MEAN TO *"STRIVE FOR SPIRITUAL MATURITY"*? _____

(Q) ANY COMMENTS ON THESES VERSES? _____

Stop and discuss the above verses and questions — Answer to questions are on the next page.

> **Philippians 3:13-14 (NASB).** [13] Brothers and sisters, I do not regard myself as having taken hold of it yet; but one thing I do: **forgetting what lies behind and reaching forward to what lies ahead,** [14] I press on toward the goal for the prize of the upward call of God in Christ Jesus.

Commentary. In these verses, Paul made two points. The first point was that he was letting go of his past and moving forward and he was not going to let his old life weigh him down. His second point was to keep his eye on the prize. Simply put, he was **not** going to let his past or the distractions of the world derail his *"upward call of God in Christ Jesus."*

Satan will try to use the believer's old life to discourage them by telling them they are not good enough for God. When a Christian falls into this trap, they forget that Jesus paid their sin debt and they have been forgiven. Paul was a murderer and was able to put that behind him because he accepted Jesus's forgiveness which allowed him to look forward toward the goal for which God had called him. Another of Satan's tricks is to keep the believer so busy they lose sight of the prize. Busyness is one of the enemies' biggest weapons.

Reflective Question: Are you so busy that you have taken your eyes off the eternal prize?

(Q) WHAT ARE OTHER WAYS SATAN TRIES TO DERAIL THE CHRISTIAN'S WALK? _____
_____

(Q) ANY COMMENTS ON THESES VERSES? _____

Stop and discuss the above verses and questions — Answer to questions are on the next page.

Answers to Questions from the Previous Page

(Q) WHAT DOES IT MEAN TO *"STRIVE FOR SPIRITUAL MATURITY"*?

- In its simplest terms, striving for spiritual maturity means becoming more like Jesus.

- This is a continuous process that will not end until we leave this life. As Paul said in verse 12, he was pressing onward toward a deeper knowledge of God.

- Spiritual maturity is learning to walk with purpose under the power of the Holy Spirit through prayer, meditation, Bible reading, service to others and fellowship with other believers. The evidence of this is the fruit of the Spirit in the believer's life.

(Q) WHAT ARE OTHER WAYS SATAN TRIES TO DERAIL THE CHRISTIAN'S WALK?

- He will try and lure believers into embracing the **pleasures of this world** with fame, money, sex, status, and reputation. Just look at the latest fad's going on today.
    - o **Selfies** are nothing more than **idolizing self**.
    - o **Social media** encourages people to **boast** about their accomplishments and exaggerate to make their lives seem more exciting or make themselves appear more attractive.
    - o The current **cancel culture** is driving believers to **compromise** their faith. Rather than taking a stand for righteousness, they straddle the fence because they are afraid. As they say, a little leaven ruins the whole dough.

- These are just some ways that Satan is using to derail the Christian's walk. How can believers avoid Satan's tricks? First, stay in communion with God through prayer and meditation. Secondly, stay in the Word through regular Bible reading and Bible study groups. And finally, rely on the power of the Holy Spirit for courage to recognize and stand against the lies of the enemy.

- The Apostle John warned us about loving the world more than we love God. *"Do not love the world nor the things in the world. If anyone loves the world, the love of the Father is not in him. For all that is in the world, the lust of the flesh and the lust of the eyes and the boastful pride of life, is not from the Father, but is from the world"* (1 John 2:15-16).

> **Philippians 3:15-16 (NASB).** [15] Therefore, all who are mature, let's have this attitude; and if in anything you have a different attitude, God will reveal that to you as well; [16] however, **let's keep living by that same standard to which we have attained**.

Commentary. Up until now, Paul has been addressing a couple of issues that were threatening to divide the church. The first threat was coming from **within the church** and was being driven by an argument between two women. The second threat was coming from **outside the church** from false teachers who were preaching a works-based salvation that was confusing the new believers. This is the same today. Satan is attacking the church from within and from external forces.

In these verses, Paul was calling **mature believers** to unite and bring the church together over the issues that were threatening to divide them. The NLT Bible said it this way, *"Let all who are spiritually mature agree on these things. If you disagree on some point, I believe God will make it plain to you. But we must hold on to the progress we have already made"* (Philippians 3:15-16 NLT).

(Q) WHAT *"INTERNAL"* ISSUES ARE THREATENING THE CHURCH TODAY? _____

(Q) WHAT *"EXTERNAL"* ISSUES ARE THREATENING THE CHURCH TODAY? _____

(Q) ANY COMMENTS ON THESES VERSES? _____

Stop and discuss the above verses and questions — Answer to questions are on the next page.

> **Philippians 3:17 (NASB).** [17] Brothers and sisters, **join in following my example**, and observe those who walk according to the pattern you have in us.

Commentary. In this verse, Paul was encouraging the Philippians to use him as a **role model** for right behavior, as well as looking to mature believers who were living out their faith. This wasn't the first time that Paul referred to himself as a role model. The NLT says it this way, *"pattern your lives after mine, and learn from those who follow our example"* (Philippians 3:17 NLT).

It takes a lot of confidence for someone to say, "look at my life, I am above reproach," which is what Paul was saying. Role models can also be great mentors. However, believers should be careful not to put mentors on a pedestal because *"all have sinned and fall short of the glory of God"* (Romans 3:23).

Reflective Question: Would your family and friends say that your life imitates Christ's life, or would they say that they can't tell the difference between your behavior and the worlds?

(Q) WHAT ARE THE BENEFITS OF HAVING A MENTOR? _____

(Q) ANY COMMENTS ON THESES VERSES? _____

Stop and discuss the above verses and questions — Answer to questions are on the next page.

Answers to Questions from the Previous Page

(Q) WHAT "*INTERNAL*" ISSUES ARE THREATENING THE CHURCH TODAY?

- One of the biggest internal problems is false teachers have infiltrated the church.

- Another problem is believers who don't take sin seriously. They claim to be Christians but their hearts are unchanged and their faith is lukewarm.

- Pastors who don't teach the whole Bible. They are more concerned with growing their congregation instead of discipling and equipping believers.

- I'm sure your group can come up with many more examples.

(Q) WHAT "*EXTERNAL*" ISSUES ARE THREATENING THE CHURCH TODAY?

- One of the biggest problems is the media painting a negative picture of Christianity that is false.

- Another big issue comes from the government trying to issue policies to hinder churches and take away their right to worship freely.

- Christians are known for what they are against, rather than for their love or all the good things they contribute to society.

- I'm sure your group can come up with many more examples.

(Q) WHAT ARE THE BENEFITS OF HAVING A MENTOR?

- There are many examples of mentoring in the Bible, here are just a few.
  - Jesus mentored and discipled the apostles, who went on to change the world.
  - Paul mentored Timothy and Titus who became pastors of their own churches.
  - Moses' father-in-law, Jethro, mentored Moses to be a great leader.

- A believer who is operating under the control of the Holy Spirit can serve as a mentor for new believers by teaching and equipping them in the ways of the Lord. Proverbs says, "*Walk with the wise and become wise; associate with fools and get in trouble*" (Proverbs 13:20 NLT).

- A mentor does not have to be a pastor or elder, they can be **anyone who is spiritually mature** in their faith.

- There are many more benefits to having a mentor which I'm sure your group came up with.

> **Philippians 3:18-19 (NASB).** [18] For many walk, of whom I often told you, and now tell you even **as I weep**, that they are the enemies of the cross of Christ, [19] whose end is destruction, **whose god is their appetite**, and whose glory is in their shame, who have their minds on earthly things.

Commentary. In the previous verses, Paul called for mature believers to help unite the church against the internal bickering that was threatening to divide the church. Now in these verses, Paul was warning the church about those who were abusing their freedom in Christ by indulging in their flesh. He described them as enemies of God "*who have their minds on earthly things.*" In other words, they were putting more value on worldly things then on their relationship with God.

The thought of some of his friends turning their back on God brought Paul to tears because he knows what is in store for people who reject Christ. Their future is eternal torment in the lake of fire. This should bring every believer to tears and motivate them to share the good news with as many people as possible. God does not condemn anyone; everyone has a choice to follow Christ or reject Him, and their decision determines their eternal resting place.

Reflective Question: Do you feel an urgency to share the Gospel with nonbelievers whose end is destruction?

(Q) WHAT DOES IT MEAN "*WHOSE GOD IS THEIR APPETITE*"? _____

(Q) ANY COMMENTS ON THESES VERSES? _____

> Stop and discuss the above verses and questions — Answer to questions are on the next page.

> **Philippians 3:20 (NASB).** [20] **For our citizenship is in heaven**, from which we also eagerly wait for a Savior, the Lord Jesus Christ.

Commentary. In the previous verses, Paul described the citizens of this world as "*enemies of God.*" Now in this verse, he reminded the believer's that there "*citizenship is in heaven.*" When a believer is born again, they are reborn into God's kingdom and are no longer citizens of this world. In Paul's second letter to the Corinthians he said, "*if anyone is in Christ, this person is a new creation; the old things passed away; behold, new things have come*" (2 Corinthians 5:17).

What a glories day it will be when Jesus returns for His people. Paul was telling the Philippians to put aside their differences and remember this world is only temporary. In other words, Christians are aliens in a foreign land and should not conform their life to the temptations of this world.

(Q) WHAT IS THE DIFFERENCE BETWEEN THE PEOPLE IN VERSES 18-19 AND THE PEOPLE IN VERSE 20? _____

(Q) ANY COMMENTS ON THESES VERSES? _____

> Stop and discuss the above verses and questions — Answer to questions are on the next page.

Answers to Questions from the Previous Page

Q) WHAT DOES IT MEAN "*WHOSE GOD IS THEIR APPETITE*"?

- This verse refers to people who "claim" to be Christians but are living a life of self-indulgence.

- They can never satisfy their appetite with the things of the world, no matter how hard they try.

- Wealth, fame, sex, materialism, alcohol, and drugs cannot bring permanent satisfaction, only God can fill this emptiness.

- They live to satisfy their fleshly desires rather than a life of self-sacrifice as Jesus taught.

(Q) WHAT IS THE DIFFERENCE BETWEEN THE PEOPLE IN VERSES 18-19 AND THE PEOPLE IN VERSE 20?

- The main difference is that in verses 18-19, Paul was describing nonbelievers "*who have their minds on earthly things.*"

- Verse 19 describes Christians who are "*citizens of heaven.*"

> **Philippians 3:21 (NASB).** [21] [Jesus] will **transform the body** of our lowly condition into conformity with **His glorious body**, by the exertion of the power that He has even to subject all things to Himself.

Commentary. Paul finished this chapter on a positive note. First, he reminded the believers that their home was in heaven, and that Jesus was in control and has power over ALL things. The Message Bible says, *"There is far more to life for us. We're citizens of high heaven. We're waiting the arrival of the Savior, the Master, Jesus Christ, who will transform our earthy bodies into glorious bodies like His own"* (Philippians 3:21 MSG).

Wow, what a great day that will be when Jesus returns. The Christians sin nature will be gone and their bodies will be transformed into new glorious bodies like Jesus's. What will this new body look like? Paul described this transformed body in his first letter to the Corinthians.

> **1 Corinthians 15:40-49, 53 (NASB).** [40] There are also **heavenly bodies** and **earthly bodies**, but the glory of the heavenly is one, and the glory of the earthly is another. [41] There is one glory of the sun, another glory of the moon, and another glory of the stars; for star differs from star in glory.
>
> [42] So also is the resurrection of the dead. It is sown a perishable body, it is raised an imperishable body; [43] it is sown in dishonor, it is raised in glory; it is sown in weakness, it is raised in power; [44] it is sown a natural body, it is raised a spiritual body. If there is a natural body, there is also a spiritual body. [45] So also it is written: *"The first man, Adam, became a living person."* The last Adam was a life-giving spirit.
>
> [46] However, the spiritual is not first, but the natural; then the spiritual. [47] The **first man** is from the earth, earthy; the **second man** is from heaven. [48] As is the earthy one, so also are those who are earthy; and as is the heavenly one, so also are those who are heavenly. [49] Just as we have borne the image of the earthy, we will also bear the image of the heavenly.
>
> [53] For this perishable must put on the imperishable, and this mortal must put on immortality.

(Q) WHAT ARE THE DIFFERENCES BETWEEN BELIEVERS "*EARTHLY BODIES*" AND THEIR "*HEAVENLY BODIES*"? _____

(Q) WHO WAS THE "*FIRST MAN*" AND WHO WAS THE "*SECOND MAN*"? _____
_____

(Q) ANY COMMENTS ON THESES VERSES? _____

Stop and discuss the above verses and questions — Answer to questions are on the next page.

Answers to Questions from the Previous Page

(Q) WHAT ARE THE DIFFERENCES BETWEEN BELIEVERS "*EARTHLY BODIES*" AND THEIR "*HEAVENLY BODIES*"?

The main difference is that earthly body is subject to decay and death, whereas the believer's heavenly body will not perish. Here are some more differences between the earthly body and the believers spiritual body awaiting them in heaven.

Earthly Body	Heavenly Body	
Perishable	Imperishable	(v. 42)
Dishonor	Glory	(v. 43)
Weak	Power	(v. 43)
Natural	Spiritual	(v. 44)
Adams image	Christ's image	(v. 49)
Mortal	Immortal	(v. 53)

(Q) WHO WAS THE "*FIRST MAN*" AND WHO WAS THE "*SECOND MAN*"?

1 Corinthians 15:47 (NASB) The **first man** is from the earth, earthy; the **second man** is from heaven.

- **The First Man**. According to Genesis, Adam was the first man (Genesis 2:7). Paul described him as having a natural body from earth.

- **The Second Man**. Jesus was the second man and is sometimes called the "second Adam" (1 Corinthians 15:49). Paul described Him as having a spiritual body from heaven.

Let's RE-Read Tonight's Verses

Philippians 3:12-21 (NASB). 12 Not that I have already grasped it all or have already become perfect,

~~~~~~

but I press on if I may also take hold of that for which I was even taken hold of by Christ Jesus.

~~~~~~

13 Brothers and sisters, I do not regard myself as having taken hold of it yet;

~~~~~~

but one thing I do: forgetting what lies behind and reaching forward to what lies ahead,

~~~~~~

14 I press on toward the goal for the prize of the upward call of God in Christ Jesus.

~~~~~~

15 Therefore, all who are mature, let's have this attitude; and if in anything you have a different attitude,

~~~~~~

God will reveal that to you as well; 16 however, let's keep living by that same standard to which we have attained.

~~~~~~

17 Brothers and sisters, join in following my example, and observe those who walk according to the pattern you have in us.

~~~~~~

18 For many walk, of whom I often told you, and now tell you even as I weep, that they are the enemies of the cross of Christ,

~~~~~~

19 whose end is destruction, whose god is their appetite, and whose glory is in their shame, who have their minds on earthly things.

~~~~~~

20 For our citizenship is in heaven, from which we also eagerly wait for a Savior, the Lord Jesus Christ;

~~~~~~

21 who will transform the body of our lowly condition into conformity with His glorious body, by the exertion of the power that He has even to subject all things to Himself.

(Q) ANY FINAL COMMENTS? _____

This is the end of this week's study.

Notes

Philippians:
Rejoice in the Lord

WEEK 7 - PHILIPPIANS 4:1-9

A Verse-by-Verse Journey through Philippians

Let's Review Last Week's Study

We finished last week with a discussion on spiritual maturity, were Paul called on the mature believers to help solve a problem in the church. He urged the Philippians to lean on the mature believers and to follow their example. He wasn't afraid to include himself by saying *"pattern your lives after mine, and learn from those who follow our example"* (Philippians 3:17 NLT). This is a model of addressing problems in the church that can still be followed today. Pastors and church elders cannot do everything nor can they address every problem. This is where mature believers can help off load their pastors by mentoring and discipling new believers.

Paul finished this chapter by grieving for those who had fallen away from their faith by indulging in their flesh. He accused them of abusing their freedom in Christ and called them enemies of God *"whose end is destruction, **whose god is their appetite**, and whose glory is in their shame, who have their minds on earthly things"* (Philippians 3:19).

(Q) WHAT DOES IT MEAN *"WHOSE GOD IS THEIR APPETITE"*? _____

(Q) ANY COMMENTS? _____

Stop and discuss the above comments and questions — Answer to questions are on the next page.

Let's Review Tonight's Study

As we finish up Paul's letter to the Philippians, it is obvious that he loved the Philippians and they loved him. Last week Paul showed his emotions by grieving for those who had fallen away from God, and tonight Paul expresses how much he misses being with his friends in Philippi. He wanted them to know how much joy it brought him when he heard how well they were doing in their Christian walk.

Then Paul addressed the conflict that was happening between two women, except this time he identified them as Euodia and Syntyche. He urged them to resolve their differences and called on several members of the church by name to help them. Later on we will use this conflict to discuss how to handle disagreements in the church.

A key verse from tonight's study is *"Do not be anxious about anything, but in everything by prayer and pleading with thanksgiving let your requests be made known to God. And the peace of God, which surpasses all comprehension, will guard your hearts and minds in Christ Jesus"* (Philippians 4:6-7).

This brings us to the final point and that is Christians should be **intentional** in what they feed their minds. The mind is a battlefield and Paul was urging the Philippians to guard their thought life against attacks from the enemy.

(Q) WHICH PIECE OF THE *"ARMOR OF GOD"* PROTECTS THE BELIEVERS *"THOUGHT LIFE"*?

_____

(Q) ANY COMMENTS? _____

Stop and discuss the above comments and questions — Answer to questions are on the next page.

Answers to Questions from the Previous Page

(Q) WHAT DOES IT MEAN "*WHOSE GOD IS THEIR APPETITE*"?

- This verse refers to people who claim to be Christians but are living a life of self-indulgence.

- They live to satisfy their fleshly desires rather than a life of self-sacrifice as Jesus taught.

- They act holy on Sundays at church, but the rest of the week they are trying to fill the God shaped hole in their soul with the things of the world.

- The Apostle John described their attitude as, "*I am rich. I have everything I want. I don't need a thing.*" In other words, they were blinded by their comfortable condition (Revelation 3:17 NLT).

(Q) WHICH PIECE OF THE "*ARMOR OF GOD*" PROTECTS THE BELIEVERS "*THOUGHT LIFE*"?

- Physically the "**helmet of salvation**" protects a soldier's head, and spiritually the helmet protects the believer's thought life.

- In addition to the helmet of salvation, the "**sword of the spirit**" represents the Word of God and it can pierce the heart and change lives.

- The Bible says, "*the Word of God is alive and powerful. It is sharper than the sharpest two-edged sword, cutting between soul and spirit, between joint and marrow. It exposes our innermost thoughts and desires*" (Hebrews 4:12 NLT).

Philippians 4:1 (NASB). [1] Therefore, my beloved brothers and sisters, whom I long to see, **my joy and crown**, stand firm in the Lord in this way, my beloved.

Commentary. Paul loved the Philippians and had a friendship with them that started ten years earlier when he visited Philippi during his second missionary journey. Since then the churches in Philippi supported Paul financially and they even sent Epaphroditus to help tend to his needs while he was imprisoned in Rome.

At the end of this verse, what did Paul mean when he said, "*stand firm in the Lord in this way*"? He was referring to the previous chapter where he (1) encouraged the Philippians to model their behavior after himself and the mature believers in the church, (2) warned the Philippians to be careful of some people in the church who were claiming to be Christians while indulging in the things of the world rather than the things of God.

(Q) WHAT DID PAUL MEAN WHEN HE CALLED THE PHILIPPIANS HIS *"JOY AND CROWN"*? _____

_____

(Q) ANY COMMENTS ON THESES VERSES? _____

Stop and discuss the above verses and questions — Answer to questions are on the next page.

Philippians 4:2 (NASB). [2] I urge **Euodia** and I urge **Syntyche** to live in harmony in the Lord.

Commentary. Finally, Paul identified the two women that were causing the division in the church. There isn't much information about Euodia and Syntyche other than they were active members of the church and were having a public spat. Paul realized that their disagreement could destroy the unity among believers, so he was forced to address them in this letter. Paul did the same thing with the church in Corinth when Chloe's people told him about a quarrel in the church. Paul wrote to the Corinthians and said "*I urge you, brothers and sisters, by the name of our Lord Jesus Christ, that you all agree and that there be no divisions among you*" (1 Corinthians 1:10). Instead of taking sides or trying to solve their problem, Paul simply encouraged them to live in harmony.

What can we learn from these women?

One thing we can learn is that even Christians who worked together in ministry can have disagreements. Another lesson is that if conflicts are not resolved quickly, they run the risk of dividing people and may destroy the witness outside the church. Remember what Jesus said, "*a house divided cannot stand.*"

(Q) HAVE YOU EVER DISAGREED WITH SOMEONE IN MINISTRY? HOW DID YOU RESOLVE THE ISSUE?

_____

(Q) ANY COMMENTS ON THESES VERSES? _____

Stop and discuss the above verses and questions — Answer to questions are on the next page.

Answers to Questions from the Previous Page

(Q) WHAT DID PAUL MEAN WHEN HE CALLED THE PHILIPPIANS HIS *"JOY AND CROWN"*?

- Paul's reference to a "crown" was one that would be presented to an athlete who has just won a race. In other words, it represented a victory or achievement.

- In that sense, Paul considered the Philippians his trophy for standing firm in the Lord, and he was proud of them because of their walk with God, and their faith brought him joy.

(Q) HAVE YOU EVER DISAGREED WITH SOMEONE IN MINISTRY? HOW DID YOU RESOLVE THE ISSUE?

- Testimony time.
- Ask for a couple of examples on resolving conflict.
- Keep the sharing to 2-3 minutes each.
- Focus the discussion away from the problem and toward the biblical resolution.

> **Philippians 4:3 (NASB).** ³ Indeed, **true companion**, I ask you also, help these women who have shared my struggle in the cause of the gospel, together with **Clement** as well as the rest of my fellow workers, whose names are in **the book of life.**

Commentary. Who was Paul referring to in this verse when he said "*true companion*"? Some people believe he was referring to Epaphroditus or maybe Timothy, the co-author of this letter. Others believe Paul was addressing this to a specific member in the Philippian church. The truth is we don't know who this was, other than they were a mature believer and were active in ministry work in the church.

In the previous verses, Paul called on the mature believers to help resolve the conflict between Euodia and Syntyche. Now in these verses, he was asking "*true companion*" and Clement to help these women. Paul set the stage for this encounter back in chapter two when he urged the Philippians to "*do nothing from selfishness or empty conceit, but with humility consider one another as more important than yourselves; do not merely look out for your own personal interests, but also for the interests of others*" (Philippians 2:3-4).

Reflective Question: Do you help people because you genuinely care about them, or do you help people so you can boast about what a good person you are?

(Q) HOW DO WE KNOW THESE WOMEN WERE "*FELLOW LABORERS*" FOR THE LORD? _____

_____

(Q) ANY COMMENTS ON THESES VERSES? _____

> **Stop and discuss the above verses and questions — Answer to questions are on the next page.**

> **Philippians 4:4-5 (NASB).** ⁴ Rejoice in the Lord always; again I will say, rejoice! ⁵ **Let your gentle spirit** be known to all people. **The Lord is near.**

Commentary. In these verses, Paul made several points. The first thing we notice is that he repeated himself by saying "*rejoice*" twice. When the Bible repeats itself, we should pay extra attention. The next thing we notice is that Paul said to rejoice "*always.*" This means believers should have **joy all the time,** even during hard times. Charles Spurgeon said "*Joy in the Lord is the cure for all discord.*" This is great advice that still applies today.

The next thing Paul did was to encourage the Philippians to have a "*gentle spirit.*" Remember, Paul was coaching the believers on how to resolve the conflict between Euodia and Syntyche and he wanted them to exercise loving kindness. The New Living Translation said "*Let everyone see that you are considerate in all you do*" (Philippians 4:5 NLT).

(Q) WHAT DID PAUL MEAN WHEN HE SAID "*THE LORD IS NEAR*"? _____

(Q) ANY COMMENTS ON THESES VERSES? _____

> **Stop and discuss the above verses and questions — Answer to questions are on the next page.**

Answers to Questions from the Previous Page

(Q) HOW DO WE KNOW THESE WOMEN WERE *"FELLOW LABORERS"* FOR THE LORD?

- Paul said, *"these women have shared **my** struggle in the cause of the gospel, together with Clement as well as the rest of my fellow workers."*

- By saying they *"these women have shared **my** struggle"*, Paul was saying they were active in the church and quite possibly may have been long time members and might have met Paul during his second missionary journey. In other words, they were fellow laborers for the Lord.

(Q) WHAT DID PAUL MEAN WHEN HE SAID *"THE LORD IS NEAR"*?

- There are several possibilities for the meaning of this verse.

  1. The Lord is omnipresent, meaning that He is always near to His people.

  2. Or it could be a reference to Jesus coming back for His church.

- In the context of the verse, the most likely meaning is the first one. Paul was reminding the Philippians to rejoice always and treat each other with gentleness because the Lord loves them and is always with them.

> **Philippians 4:6 (NASB).** [6] Do not be anxious about **anything**, but in **everything** by prayer and pleading with thanksgiving let your requests be made known to God.

Commentary. Simply put, believers should pray for "*everything*" and should not worry about "*anything*." That's a tall order. Can any of us say we have never worried, or always prayed when faced with a difficult situation? I certainly can't. Let's look at this verse in context with the previous verses. When we do that, it means Christians should not be worried about pushing their own agenda, but instead, they should make their needs known to God through prayer, and then trust in Him for the results.

Some people have used this verse as a model for prayer by turning it into an acronym called A.C.T.S. which stands for: **A**ffirm – **C**onfess – **T**hanks – **S**upplication. If you have never heard this acronym, it is a simple way to bring your petitions to the Lord. Of course, believers don't need an acronym to talk to God.

Reflective Question: How is my prayer life? Have I made spending time with God a priority?

(Q) CAN YOU EXPAND AND DESCRIBE PRAYING USING A.C.T.S.? _____

(Q) ANY COMMENTS ON THESES VERSES? _____

Stop and discuss the above verses and questions — Answer to questions are on the next page.

> **Philippians 4:7 (NASB).** [7] And the peace of God, which surpasses all comprehension, will guard your hearts and minds in Christ Jesus.

Commentary. One of God's promises to His people is that if they take their worries and petitions to Him, they can experience the "*peace of God, which surpasses all comprehension.*" God's peace is not of this world and is beyond human understanding. As the Apostle John said, "*Peace I leave you, My peace I give you; **not as the world gives**, do I give to you. Do not let your hearts be troubled, nor fearful*" (John 14:27).

One thing is certain, worry will destroy God's peace in a hurry. What's that old saying, "if you worry - why pray, and if you pray - why worry." In other words, if you choose to focus on your problems, then you are choosing to worry, and in turn, you are choosing to push God out. However, if you choose to pray and bring your troubles to Him, He promises to draw near to you and bring you His peace (James 4:8).

Many people today live lives of self-gratification and self-sufficiency. Others have a tendency to be "control freaks." What does that mean? It means that some people have a hard time letting go and letting God, consequentially, they miss out on experiencing God's peace.

Reflective Question: Are you a worry wart? Do you have your eyes on your problems rather than God?

(Q) WHAT DOES IT MEAN TO "*GUARD YOUR HEARTS AND MINDS IN CHRIST JESUS*"? _____
_____

(Q) ANY COMMENTS ON THESES VERSES? _____

Stop and discuss the above verses and questions — Answer to questions are on the next page.

Answers to Questions from the Previous Page

(Q) CAN YOU EXPAND AND DESCRIBE PRAYING USING A.C.T.S.?

As with all prayers, Christians must submit to God's will, as in "*not my will, but Thy will be done*" (Matthew 26:39). Remember that prayer is an act of worship. It is recognizing God for who He is and what He has done, rather than focusing on ourselves.

- **A**ffirm. Praise God and affirm or acknowledge that He is the Lord of your life and the creator of the universe.

- **C**onfess. Admit your faults and ask for forgiveness.

- **T**hanks. Show your appreciation by thanking God for what He has done in your life and for what He is going to do in the future.

- **S**upplication. Only after you have affirmed God and confessed your sins, should you make your request or petitions known to Him.

(Q) WHAT DOES IT MEAN TO "*GUARD YOUR HEARTS AND MINDS IN CHRIST JESUS*"?

- Simply put, without God, a believer cannot truly experience and maintain peace. It is God who brings peace and **protects** the believer's hearts and minds from the worries of this world.

- One of the pieces of the armor of God is the Helmet of Salvation. The helmet protects the soldier's head during battle, and spiritually, the helmet guards the believer's **thought life**. Paul knew the mind was a battlefield, and he was urging the Philippians to guard their thought life against attacks from the enemy.

- The Message Bible says it this way, "*It's wonderful what happens when Christ displaces worry at the center of your life.*" (Philippians 4:7 MSG).

- Here is some bumper sticker wisdom: "No God–No Peace, Know God–Know Peace."

> **Philippians 4:8-9 (NASB).** [8] Finally, brothers and sisters, whatever is **true**, whatever is **honorable**, whatever is **right**, whatever is **pure**, whatever is **lovely**, whatever is **commendable**, if there is any **excellence** and if anything **worthy of praise**, think about these things. [9] As for the things you have learned and received and heard and seen in me, **practice these things**, and the God of peace will be with you.

Commentary. In today's world, we are being bombarded every day with hundreds of commercials and advertisement's promising happiness and fulfillment. But don't be fooled, for the things of this world can only bring temporary pleasure.

Solomon was the richest and wisest man who ever lived, and this is what he had to say about trying to find happiness from this world: *"Those who love money will never have enough. How meaningless to think that wealth brings true happiness"* (Ecclesiastes 5:10 NLT). Even Jesus warned against being materialistic when He told the crowds, *"Guard against every kind of greed. Life is not measured by how much you own"* (Luke 12:15 NLT).

As Paul brought his letter to a close, he was reminding the Philippians to watch what they feed their minds. It's like that old saying, "garbage in – garbage out." Paul was encouraging the believers to imitate his behavior and to apply the things he mentioned into their daily lives. This is great advice for believers today. Be **intentional** in what you feed your mind and how you respond to adversity. Ask God to help you focus on what is good and pure. If Christians choose to practice the things Paul mentioned, they will have peace that surpasses all understanding, and will produce the **fruit of the Spirit** in their lives.

Reflective Question: Are you feeding your mind with the temporary things of the world or with the eternal Word of God?

(Q) WHAT IS THE *"FRUIT OF THE SPIRIT"*? _____

(Q) ANY COMMENTS ON THESES VERSES? _____

Stop and discuss the above verses and questions — Answer to questions are on the next page.

(Q) WHAT IS THE "*FRUIT OF THE SPIRIT*"?

- The fruit of the Spirit are produced in believers when they allow the Holy Spirit to guide their lives and consist of "*love, joy, peace, patience, kindness, goodness, faithfulness, gentleness, self-control; against such things there is no law*" (Galatians 5:22-23).

- Paul was encouraging the Philippians to focus on whatever is true, honorable, right, pure, lovely, commendable, and excellence so that they would be more like Christ (Philippians 4:8).

Let's RE-Read Tonight's Verses

Philippians 4:1-9 (NASB). [1] Therefore, my beloved brothers and sisters, whom I long to see, my joy and crown, stand firm in the Lord in this way, my beloved.

~~~~~~

[2] I urge Euodia and I urge Syntyche to live in harmony in the Lord.

~~~~~~

[3] Indeed, true companion, I ask you also, help these women who have shared my struggle in the cause of the gospel,

~~~~~~

together with Clement as well as the rest of my fellow workers, whose names are in the book of life.

~~~~~~

[4] Rejoice in the Lord always; again I will say, rejoice! [5] Let your gentle spirit be known to all people. The Lord is near.

~~~~~~

[6] Do not be anxious about anything, but in everything by prayer and pleading with thanksgiving let your requests be made known to God.

~~~~~~

[7] And the peace of God, which surpasses all comprehension, will guard your hearts and minds in Christ Jesus.

~~~~~~

[8] Finally, brothers and sisters, whatever is true, whatever is honorable, whatever is right, whatever is pure, whatever is lovely, whatever is commendable,

~~~~~~

if there is any excellence and if anything worthy of praise, think about these things.

~~~~~~

[9] As for the things you have learned and received and heard and seen in me, practice these things, and the God of peace will be with you.

(Q) ANY FINAL COMMENTS? _____

This is the end of this week's study.

Notes

Philippians:
Rejoice in the Lord

WEEK 8 - PHILIPPIANS 4:10-23

Let's Review Last Week's Study

Last week Paul identified Euodia and Syntyche as the women who were causing strife and division in the church at Philippi. They were believers who worked together in "*the cause of the gospel*" which meant they were partners in ministry work. Paul urged Clement and "*true companion*" to help these women resolve their issues. Who was "*true companion*"? Some people believe he was Epaphroditus or maybe Timothy, the co-author of this letter. The truth is we don't know who this was. Paul also urged those whose names are in the "*book of life*" to help these women resolve their issue. In other words, he was asking everyone in the church to prevent this from dividing them and to resolve this peacefully.

A key verse from last week was "*Do not be anxious about anything, but in everything by prayer and pleading with thanksgiving let your requests be made known to God. And the peace of God, which surpasses all comprehension, will guard your hearts and minds in Christ Jesus*" (Philippians 4:6-7). Another name for anxious is **worry**. If you choose to focus on your problems, then you are choosing to worry which will push God out. However, if you choose to pray and bring your troubles to Him, He promises to draw near to you and bring you His peace which surpasses all understanding.

This brings us to Paul's final point. Christians should be **intentional** in what they feed their minds. Paul recognized that the mind is a battlefield and he was urging the Philippians to guard their thought life against attacks from the enemy.

(Q) WHAT DOES IT MEAN TO "*GUARD YOUR HEARTS AND MIND IN CHRIST JESUS*"? _____
_____

(Q) ANY COMMENTS ON THESES VERSES? _____

Stop and discuss the above comments and questions — Answer to questions are on the next page.

Let's Review Tonight's Study

Tonight, we will finish Philippians with Paul thanking them for their financial support. We will also discuss one of the most quoted verses in the Bible, which is "*I know how to get along with little, and I also know how to live in prosperity; in any and every circumstance **I have learned the secret of being filled** and going hungry, both of having abundance and suffering need. I can do all things through Him who strengthens me*" (Philippians 4:12-13). Notice what Paul said about the "*secret of being filled,*" or as some Bible translations say, "*the secret of contentment.*" According to Paul, contentment is not a normal state for humans because it must be **learned**. We'll discuss what this means in tonight's study.

Paul concluded his letter by sending greetings from all the believers in Rome, especially from those in the house of Caesar. Why did he specifically mention the believers in the house of Caesar? We'll find out later on in tonight's study.

Reflective Question: Am I content with God's blessings, or do I grumble because I think it's not enough?

(Q) ANY COMMENTS ON THESES VERSES? _____

Stop and discuss the above comments.

Answers to Questions from the Previous Page

(Q) WHAT DOES IT MEAN TO "*GUARD YOUR HEARTS AND MIND IN CHRIST JESUS*"?

- Simply put, without God, a believer cannot truly experience and maintain peace. It is God who brings peace and **protects** the believer's hearts and minds from the worries of this world.

- One of the pieces of the armor of God is the Helmet of Salvation. The helmet protects the soldier's head during battle, and spiritually, the helmet protects the believer's **thought life**. Paul knew the mind was a battlefield, and he was urging the Philippians to guard their thought life against attacks from the enemy.

- The Message Bible says it this way, "*It's wonderful what happens when Christ displaces worry at the center of your life.*" (Philippians 4:7 MSG).

Let's Begin Tonight's Study

> **Philippians 4:10 (NASB).** [10] But I rejoiced in the Lord greatly, that now at last **you have revived your concern for me**; indeed, you were concerned before, but you lacked an opportunity to act.

Commentary. One of the reasons for Paul's letter was to thank the Philippians for sending him money with Epaphroditus. Paul was rejoicing for the provisions and for the help that Epaphroditus provided him by staying in Rome.

When Paul said "*at last*," it leads us to believe the Philippians financial support came later than he expected. Paul gives us a hint as to why they were late when he said they "*lacked an opportunity.*" We are not sure if this meant the Philippians did not have someone available to deliver the funds, or they did not have the resources and had to wait until the funds were available. In either case, Paul was expressing his gratitude for the Philippians support. You might say that Epaphroditus was on a missionary trip.

Reflective Question: Do you support missionaries financially and through prayer?

(Q) HAVE YOU EVER BEEN ON A "*SHORT-TERM MISSION TRIP*"? DESCRIBE YOUR EXPERIENCE.

_____

(Q) ANY COMMENTS ON THESES VERSES? _____

Stop and discuss the above comments and questions — Answer to questions are on the next page.

> **Philippians 4:11 (NASB).** [11] Not that I speak from need, for I have **learned** to be content in whatever circumstances I am.

Commentary. Notice what Paul said about contentment. He said he has "*learned*" to be content, which implies contentment is not a normal state for him or for us. We are so busy working and trying to climb the corporate ladder that we don't stop to enjoy the blessings all around us. Our society suffers from a disease called "more." If only I had more money, or more clothes, or more vacations, or more stuff, then I'll be happy. I just need more.

Paul was content even though he was on house arrest in Rome for a crime he did not commit. How is this possible? Most people would be angry and bitter for being wrongly punished, but not Paul. He had learned to be content no matter his circumstances. How can we learn to be content like Paul?

Reflective Question: Are you satisfied with the life that God has given you, or do you suffer from the disease of more, just give me more.

(Q) WHAT IS THE SECRET FOR LIVING A LIFE OF CONTENTMENT? _____

(Q) ANY COMMENTS ON THESES VERSES? _____

Stop and discuss the above verses and questions — Answer to questions are on the next page.

Answers to Questions from the Previous Page

(Q) HAVE YOU EVER BEEN ON A "*SHORT-TERM MISSION TRIP*"? DESCRIBE YOUR EXPERIENCE.

- Testimony time.

- If someone in your group has been on a mission trip, have them describe the pros and cons of their trip.

- Try and keep the sharing to 3-4 minutes.

(Q) WHAT IS THE SECRET FOR LIVING A LIFE OF CONTENTMENT?

- The main key is to keep your eyes on the Lord rather than your circumstances.

- Another key is gratitude. When was the last time you took some time to appreciate God's blessings, and then thank Him for providing for your needs and many of your wants?

- As Paul said earlier, believers should practice praying and bringing their worries to Him and then trusting that all things will work out according to His plans.

- When believers consistently pray and spend time in fellowship with the Lord, they **learn** to trust Him in prosperous times and in hard times which leads to contentment.

> **Philippians 4:12-13 (NASB).** ¹² I know how to get along with little, and I also know how to live in prosperity; in any and every circumstance I have learned the secret of being filled and going hungry, both of having abundance and suffering need. ¹³ **I can do all things through Him who strengthens me**.

Commentary. These verses contain one of the most quoted verses in all of the Bible which is, "*I can do all things through Him who strengthens me*" (v.13). What does this verse mean in context with the previous verses? To help us understand it, let's look at Paul's past life as Saul of Tarsus.

Saul was a respected Jew who came from a well to do family. He was a Roman citizen which meant he enjoyed all the privileges that came with being a Roman. He trained under the Rabbi Gamaliel and was a highly educated Pharisee who was a member of the Sanhedrin Council. In other words, Paul knew "*how to live in prosperity*," but gave up everything and walked away from that life when Jesus called him. As a follower of Christ, Paul knew "*how to get along with little*." Now that we understand the context of this verse, what does it mean?

(Q) WHAT DOES VERSE 13 MEAN IN RELATION TO VERSE 12? _____

(Q) ANY COMMENTS ON THESES VERSES? _____

> **Stop and discuss the above verses and questions — Answer to questions are on the next page.**

> **Philippians 4:14-17 (NASB).** ¹⁴ Nevertheless, **you have done well to share with me in my difficulty**. ¹⁵ You yourselves also know, Philippians, that at the first preaching of the gospel, after I left Macedonia, no church shared with me in the matter of giving and receiving except you alone; ¹⁶ for even in Thessalonica you sent a gift more than once for my needs. ¹⁷ **Not that I seek the gift itself, but I seek the profit which increases to your account**.

Commentary. The word "nevertheless" is a connecting word, and in this case, Paul was linking his wrongful imprisonment with the Philippians sacrifice to send money to help ease his suffering. In other words, **the Philippians were sharing in Paul's suffering by sacrificially giving to him**.

Paul didn't stop there as he continued to thank the Philippians for other times they sent him financial support. Does this mean the Philippians were the only ones who helped Paul? No, that's not what this means. Paul was referring to two specific events where the Philippians were the only ones who provided support; however, there were other times when Paul received financial support from other churches.

Reflective Question: Do you give out of your abundance or sacrificially? Do you give with a joyful heart or reluctantly?

(Q) WHAT DID PAUL MEAN WHEN HE SAID "*I SEEK THE PROFIT WHICH INCREASES TO YOUR ACCOUNT*"? _____

(Q) ANY COMMENTS ON THESES VERSES? _____

> **Stop and discuss the above verses and questions — Answer to questions are on the next page.**

Answers to Questions from the Previous Page

(Q) WHAT DOES VERSE 13 MEAN IN RELATION TO VERSE 12?

- Paul was saying that no matter his circumstances, God will give him the strength to persevere through life's difficulties.

- Some false teachers use this verse to preach a prosperity gospel claiming that God will financially bless them. That's not what these verses mean.

- In fact, Paul taught the opposite. He said that Christians will experience persecution for their faith, but God will give them what they need to endure hard times.

- Whether you are going through a time of plenty or a time of want, turn to God and He will give you the strength to endure and live a life of contentment no matter your circumstances.

(Q) WHAT DID PAUL MEAN WHEN HE SAID "*I SEEK THE PROFIT WHICH INCREASES TO YOUR ACCOUNT*"?

- Paul was grateful for the Philippians support; however, he was happier for the eternal blessing God would bestow on them for their generosity. This was **not** an earthly blessing, but rather a **heavenly treasure** that Jesus described when He said, "*Do not store up for yourselves treasures on earth, where moth and rust destroy, and where thieves break in and steal. But store up for yourselves treasures in heaven, where neither moth nor rust destroys, and where thieves do not break in or steal; for where your treasure is, there your heart will be also*" (Matthew 6:19-21).

- Another way to look at this verse is to compare it to the law of sowing and reaping, which is mentioned several times in the Bible. Here is one example: "*I say this: the one who sows sparingly will also reap sparingly, and the one who sows generously will also reap generously*" (2 Corinthians 9:6).

- The bottom line is that God is generous and wants to bless His children, and it pleases Him when His people are also generous. As Jesus said, "*Give, and it will be given to you*" (Luke 6:38).

> **Philippians 4:18 (NASB).** [18] I have received everything in full and have an abundance; I am amply supplied, having received from Epaphroditus what you have sent, **a fragrant aroma**, an acceptable sacrifice, pleasing to God.

Commentary. Paul was thanking the Philippians for their generosity because they had given him everything he needed and more. He called their gifts a *"fragrant aroma"* which was a reference to the Old Testament where **burnt offerings** were considered a sweet aroma to God. The Bible mentions the Law of Burnt Offers in Leviticus chapters 1-7. The offerings were done in **obedience to God** and were supposed to **costs the giver something**. They are described as *"an aroma pleasing to the Lord"* (Leviticus 1:9).

We know that the Philippians gave sacrificially to Paul because in his second letter to the Corinthians he wrote: *"I can testify that [the Philippians] gave not only what they could afford, but far more. And they did it of their own free will"* (2 Corinthians 8:3 NLT).

This brings up an interesting question regarding giving to the church. Is tithing still required, or is it an Old Testament decree that is obsolete?

(Q) IS TITHING *"A COMMANDMENT"* IN THE NEW TESTAMENT? _____

(Q) ANY COMMENTS ON THESES VERSES? _____

> **Stop and discuss the above verses and questions — Answer to questions are on the next page.**

> **Philippians 4:19-20 (NASB).** [19] And my God will supply **all your needs** according to His riches in glory in Christ Jesus. [20] Now to our God and Father be the glory forever and ever. Amen.

Commentary. Paul knew the Philippians financial gifts were a sacrifice for them and he was reassuring them that God would supply all their needs for their generosity. Charles Spurgeon said it this way, *"You have helped me out of your deep poverty, taking from your scanty store; but my God shall supply all your need out of His riches in glory."*

Paul ended this section by worshipping God by acknowledging His glory as God the Father. By ending with *"Amen,"* he was saying, *"let it be so"* that God will supply all your needs.

Reflective Question: Do I live my life in faith believing that God will supply all my needs or do I live in fear?

(Q) WHAT IS THE DIFFERENCE BETWEEN OUR *"WANTS"* AND OUR *"NEEDS"*? _____

_____

(Q) ANY COMMENTS ON THESES VERSES? _____

> **Stop and discuss the above verses and questions — Answer to questions are on the next page.**

Answers to Questions from the Previous Page

(Q) IS TITHING "*A COMMANDMENT*" IN THE NEW TESTAMENT?

- Let's look at the history of tithing before we answer this question. The concept of tithing was part of the Law requiring the Israelites to give 10 percent of their crops and livestock to the temple priest (Leviticus 27:30-33).

- There were actually several tithes mentioned in the Old Testament, totaling over 20 percent of their crops and livestock (Numbers 18:26).

- When Jesus died on the cross, He fulfilled the Law, thus eliminating the legalistic system of tithing.

- Now that we understand where tithing started, let's look at the New Testament for the answer.

- The concept of tithing is not in the New Testament and neither is the idea of giving 10 percent.

- However, the New Testament does encourage believers to support their spiritual leaders in accordance to what they can afford (1 Corinthians 16:2).

- Above all, when you give, give with a cheerful heart (2 Corinthians 9:7), and don't go boasting about how much you gave (Matthew 6:3).

- One time I asked a pastor if tithing 10 percent was biblical. He responded, "*no, you are free to give more than 10 percent if you like.*"

(Q) WHAT IS THE DIFFERENCE BETWEEN OUR "*WANTS*" AND OUR "*NEEDS*"?

Wants

- These are things that are **not** needed for sustaining life. In short, "our wants" are things used for self-gratification and pleasure.

- The Bible describes these as "*living in accordance with the flesh*" (Romans 8:12-13).

- The flesh can never be satisfied and has an unquenchable appetite.

Needs

- These are the basic necessities required for life, such as: water, food, oxygen, sun, clothing for warmth, sex for procreation.

- Some people include love, friendship, exercise, laughter, safety, and money for purchasing food and water.

- Christians would put their relationship with Jesus Christ as their highest need. Jesus said, "*Man shall not live on bread alone, but on every word that comes out of the mouth of God*" (Matthew 3:4).

> **Philippians 4:21 (NASB).** ²¹ Greet every **saint** in Christ Jesus. The **brothers** who are with me greet you.

Commentary. Paul concluded his letter by sending greetings to all the believers in Philippi. He called the Christians in Philippi "*saints*" which he often did in his letters. We discussed this at the beginning of this study, but as a reminder, the Hebrew word for saint is Hagios which means to be **set apart by God**. All Christians have been set apart because of the righteousness they received when Jesus went to the cross and atoned for their sins. Paul also sent greetings from the brothers who were with him.

Reflective Question: Do you live your life set apart for Christ?

(Q) WHO WERE THE BROTHERS WITH PAUL IN ROME? _____

(Q) ANY COMMENTS ON THESES VERSES? _____

Stop and discuss the above verses and questions — Answer to questions are on the next page.

> **Philippians 4:22-23 (NASB).** ²² All the saints greet you, **especially those of Caesar's household**. ²³ The grace of the Lord Jesus Christ be with **your spirit**.

Commentary. Paul finished his letter by mentioning all the believers in Rome send their greetings, especially the believers of "*Caesar's household*." Then he ended his letter the same way he started it by sending the grace of the Lord to be with the Philippians. The Message Bible says it this way, "*Receive and experience the amazing grace of the Master, Jesus Christ, deep, deep within yourselves*" (Philippians 4:23 MSG).

Verse 23 implies there is a difference between the human spirit, which Paul calls "*your spirit*," and the Holy Spirit. Do humans have a spirit separate from the Holy Spirit? Let's look to the Bible for the answer. In the book of Job, Elihu, son of Barakel said, "*there is **a spirit within people**, the breath of the Almighty within them, that makes them intelligent*" (Job 32:8 NLT). And in Romans Paul wrote, "*The Spirit Himself testifies with **our spirit** that we are children of God*" (Romans 8:16).

So the answer is yes, humans have a spirit separate from the Holy Spirit. Therefore, Paul was praying for the grace of God to be with the Philippians human spirit.

(Q) WHY DID PAUL SPECIFICALLY MENTION THE "*SAINTS IN CAESAR'S HOUSEHOLD*" SEND THEIR GREETINGS? _____

_____

(Q) ANY COMMENTS ON THESES VERSES? _____

Stop and discuss the above verses and questions — Answer to questions are on the next page.

Answers to Questions from the Previous Page

(Q) WHO WERE THE BROTHERS WITH PAUL IN ROME?

- **Epaphroditus**. He delivered supplies and money to Paul from the churches in Philippi, and then stayed in Rome to help take care of Paul. His self-sacrifice and devotion to Paul led him to get seriously sick and almost die. After he recovered, Paul sent him home and had him deliver this letter to the Philippians.

- **Timothy**. He was in Rome and co-authored Philippians with Paul (Philippians 1:1). Paul was planning on sending Timothy from Rome to Philippi (Philippians 2:19).

- **Doctor Luke**. He traveled with Paul and was in Rome to help tend to his medical needs. We know this because Luke wrote, "***We** boarded an Adramyttian ship that was about to sail to the regions along the coast of Asia*" (Acts 27:2). By saying "*we,*" he was referring to Paul and himself as the author of Acts. They were about to board a ship to take them to Rome for Paul's trial in front of the Emperor Nero.

EXTRA CREDIT. We haven't mentioned these believers, but they were also with Paul in Rome. If you knew this, you get extra credit for being a biblical scholar.

- **Tychicus**. We met Tychicus during our study on Acts when he traveled with Paul on his third missionary journey to deliver monetary gifts to the churches in Jerusalem (Acts 20:3-4, Romans 15:25-26). Then later on, he delivered letters from Paul to the Colossians and to the Ephesians (Colossians 4:7-8, Ephesians 6:21). He was in Rome when Paul sent him to Ephesus as a temporary pastor so that Timothy could come to Rome and visit Paul (2 Timothy 4:12).

- **Aristarchus**. We first met Aristarchus in Ephesus when he accompanied Paul to Syria (Acts 20:1-6). He traveled with Paul and Luke to Rome as a prisoner (Acts 27:1-2).

(Q) WHY DID PAUL SPECIFICALLY MENTION THE "*SAINTS IN CAESAR'S HOUSEHOLD*" SEND THEIR GREETINGS?

- Paul was on house arrest and chained to a Roman soldier 24 hours a day. The soldiers were rotated every six hours allowing Paul to preach to the entire regiment of the Roman army.

- One by one, Caesars army heard the good news and accepted Jesus as their Lord and Savior.

- Paul wanted the Philippians to know that his wrongful imprisonment has led to the conversion of the entire Roman army and they were now brothers in Christ. *Selah*.

Let's RE-Read Tonight's Verses

Philippians 4:10-23 (NASB). [10] But I rejoiced in the Lord greatly, that now at last you have revived your concern for me; indeed, you were concerned before, but you lacked an opportunity to act.
~~~~~~
[11] Not that I speak from need, for I have learned to be content in whatever circumstances I am.
~~~~~~
[12] I know how to get along with little, and I also know how to live in prosperity;
~~~~~~
in any and every circumstance I have learned the secret of being filled and going hungry, both of having abundance and suffering need.
~~~~~~
[13] I can do all things through Him who strengthens me. [14] Nevertheless, you have done well to share with me in my difficulty.
~~~~~~
[15] You yourselves also know, Philippians, that at the first preaching of the gospel, after I left Macedonia,
~~~~~~
no church shared with me in the matter of giving and receiving except you alone;
~~~~~~
[16] for even in Thessalonica you sent a gift more than once for my needs.
~~~~~~
[17] Not that I seek the gift itself, but I seek the profit which increases to your account.
~~~~~~
[18] But I have received everything in full and have an abundance;
~~~~~~
I am amply supplied, having received from Epaphroditus what you have sent, a fragrant aroma, an acceptable sacrifice, pleasing to God.
~~~~~~
[19] And my God will supply all your needs according to His riches in glory in Christ Jesus.
~~~~~~
[20] Now to our God and Father be the glory forever and ever. Amen.
~~~~~~
[21] Greet every saint in Christ Jesus. The brothers who are with me greet you. [22] All the saints greet you, especially those of Caesar's household.
~~~~~~
[23] The grace of the Lord Jesus Christ be with your spirit.

(Q) ANY FINAL COMMENTS? _____

This is the end of this week's study.

Congratulations, you have completed the study on Paul's letter to the Philippians.

Notes

REFERENCES

The Apostle Paul's Letters

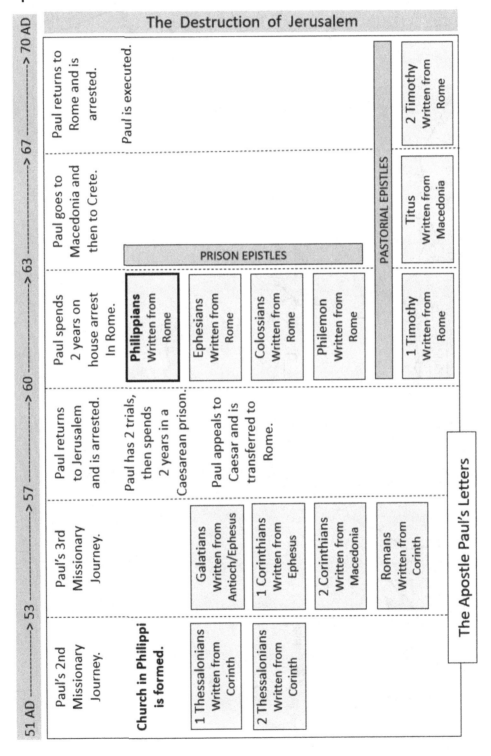

The Destruction of Jerusalem

51 AD → 53	→ 57	→ 60	→ 63	→ 67	→ 70 AD
Paul's 2nd Missionary Journey.	Paul's 3rd Missionary Journey.	Paul returns to Jerusalem and is arrested. Paul has 2 trials, then spends 2 years in a Caesarean prison. Paul appeals to Caesar and is transferred to Rome.	Paul spends 2 years on house arrest In Rome.	Paul goes to Macedonia and then to Crete.	Paul returns to Rome and is arrested. *Paul is executed.*
Church in Philippi is formed.					

PRISON EPISTLES

- **Philippians** Written from Rome
- Ephesians Written from Rome
- Colossians Written from Rome
- Philemon Written from Rome

PASTORIAL EPISTLES

- 1 Timothy Written from Rome
- Titus Written from Macedonia
- 2 Timothy Written from Rome

- Galatians Written from Antioch/Ephesus
- 1 Corinthians Written from Ephesus
- 2 Corinthians Written from Macedonia
- Romans Written from Corinth

- 1 Thessalonians Written from Corinth
- 2 Thessalonians Written from Corinth

The Apostle Paul's Letters

Map of Paul's 2nd Missionary Journey

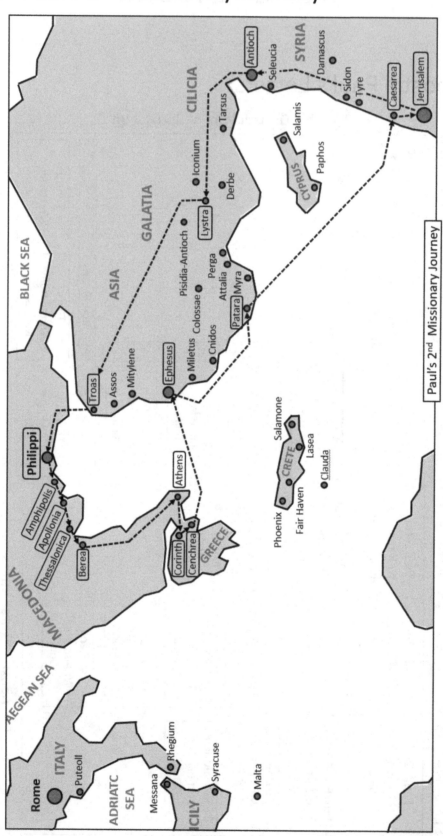

Map of Paul's Journey to Rome

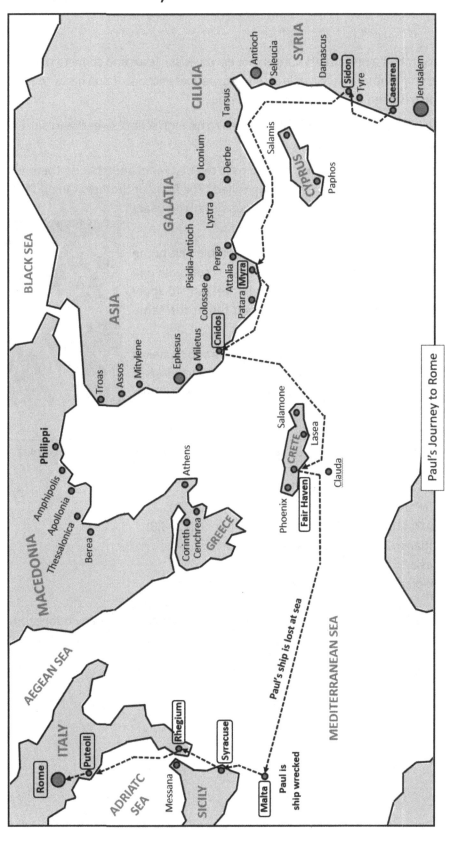

ABOUT THE AUTHOR

Ralph Robert Gomez is a retired software engineer who loves Jesus and came to the Lord later in life. At the age of thirty-nine years old, while attending graduate school, Ralph had a "*road to Damascus*" experience and has been walking with the Lord since.

Ralph is a native of Colorado and has been married to his high school sweetheart since 1975 and has two children and three grandchildren.

Ralph has been writing Bible studies for the past twenty years and sharing them with his home group, "*The James Gang*" and a men's group called "*The Band of Brothers.*" In addition, Ralph and his wife have hosted numerous marriage groups over the years and have a passion for helping marriages succeed.

At the urging of his friends and family, Ralph assembled his home group studies into a series of Precept Bible Studies that challenge the reader to probe deep into God's Word (interpret) and to apply it to their daily lives (application), while having fun at the same time!

Ralph's background as an engineer, writing software and technical documents, has uniquely qualified him to use his *analytical skills* to dissect God's Word, verse by verse, making it easy and simple to understand.

Here are other precept Bible studies available from Ralph Robert Gomez.

Acts: The Birth of the Church (ch 1-12)
Acts: Paul's Three Missionary Journeys (ch 13-21)
Acts: Paul's Arrest, Trial and Imprisonment (ch 21-28)
Galatians: Oh, You Foolish Galatians
Ephesians: The Queen of the Epistles
Philippians: Rejoice in the Lord

All books are available at **www.ralphrobertgomez.com** or any book store

---

Printed in the United States
by Baker & Taylor Publisher Services